KNOWLEDGE
THROUGH
COLOR

MOTORCYCLES
BY PHIL SCHILLING
PHOTOGRAPHS BY BILL DELANEY

A RIDGE PRESS BOOK/BANTAM BOOKS
TORONTO   NEW YORK   LONDON

Photo Credits

Bill Delaney—all photographs except the following:
Bruce Finlayson: 22, 23;
Jan Hesse: 142, 143, 144, 145, 149, 151, 152, 154-155;
Vince Lisanti: 34, 35;
Courtesy Norton Triumph Corporation: 36-37;
Courtesy Yamaha International Corporation: 17.

Title Page—Norton 850 John Player Special

Contents

Modern Classics

Classic motorcycles are machines which have gone to legend. Most motorcycles readily tumble into the blankness of an unrecalled past. Only a few models escape that yawning anonymity and become lodged in the sport's history. The reasons are varied: the way certain motorcycles performed or looked or felt; the technical achievements they represented; the new directions in which they propelled the sport. But all great motorcycles share one common denominator; they make motorcyclists spark with excitement.

Early classics do not have a direct connection to contemporary motorcycles. Hand oil pumps, cylinder-head priming cocks, leaf-spring front forks and other technology from the twenties and thirties hardly link up with the motorcycles of the seventies. Conversely, most modern classics were built in the late fifties and through the sixties. Any present-day enthusiast would recognize the major design elements—telehydraulic forks, swinging-arm rear suspension, adequate brakes and powerful, compact engines. Today's motorcyclist could immediately operate a 1960 Honda Super Hawk, but that same fellow would be baffled by a 1925 Indian Scout.

To some enthusiasts, the machines of the fifties and sixties may seem too contemporary to be properly legendary. This is not the case. Forty-five years of motorcycle development have been compressed in the last two decades. In 1955 motorcycle engineering appeared remarkably crude and primitive compared to automobiles. And why not—the last era of intense, creative motorcycle development ended in the twenties. But by 1975 motorcycles had caught up with, and in some cases surpassed, automobiles as sophisticated vehicles. That was no wonder. Motorcycling flowered in the sixties as manufacturers introduced hundreds of new motorcycles in a decade of amazing activity. And some truly remarkable modern classics were part of that flowering.

4

*With its grace of line and form, the
Triumph Bonneville was the most handsome
statement of the British vertical twin.*

BSA Gold Star

Most modern classics pointed forward. As harbingers of the future, such classics connect directly to contemporary machines. The lineage between the Honda CB-77 and present-day Honda roadsters proceeds in an orderly path.

Other classics intersect with contemporary motorcycling in a different way. The BSA Gold Star was the perfect expression of the big-single-cylinder motorcycle: light, narrow, agile, simple multi-duty machinery. More than a decade after the last real Gold Star was built, the concept of the big single remains an attractive idea in motorcycling.

The Gold Star was a universal motorcycle. Americans raced them on flat tracks, Europeans ran the big single in road races, others used the Gold Star for trials, and the motorcycle served many owners everywhere as a road bike.

BSA first introduced their historic 500cc single-cylinder motorcycle in 1938; a second series 350cc/500cc bike débuted in 1949–50; and the final revision reached the marketplace in 1954. Physically, the Gold Star was a large motorcycle. From the beginning BSA scaled the bike as a full 500. Unlike modern big singles (350–450 two- and four-strokes), the BSA Gold Star wasn't a pumped-up 250 or 350. The majestic old bike had a long-stroke, undersquare engine. Its 85mm piston travelled up and down 88mm strokes. Though the real Gold Star died in 1963, BSA later applied the label to a smaller, lighter single. But that ersatz Gold Star never had the charisma of the original bikes.

The Gold Star had a purposeful grace born of its simplicity. At speed, the engine emitted great thumping sounds, mellowed and rounded in its silencer. Snapping the throttle shut reversed the thumps into a lazy, gutteral yawn. The noises were truly lovely. Perhaps that's half the magic of the big thump-and-yawn singles.

6

Owners may make detailed changes in their Gold Stars—but the big thumping single cylinder remains the center of it all.

BMW R60

Not all machines were fast, boisterous vehicles before the Japanese revolution in motorcycling. The sport always had a strain of civil machines, and BMW built refined motorcycles. All German motorcycles of the post-war period were "gentlemen's motorcycles," if one assumed that gentlemen would prefer silent, smooth, and finely crafted conveyances which were a bit shy on horsepower but very long indeed on reliability.

Most popular of the BMW models were the R60 and R69S opposed twins. These 600cc, overhead-valve, pushrod twins had 35 and 42 horsepower respectively. The R69S was the tuned-up version of the basic 600cc touring bike; but even so, the R69S could not touch the quickest British and American models. On the other hand, the BMW **8** clientele never worshipped drag-strip clocks as the final measure of a

machine. To them reliability was far more important.

Owners of the German twins prized the BMW one-kick starting. One-kick starting was a big thing in the 1950's, and almost a BMW monopoly. BMW's shaft-drive was also an endearing feature. Enthusiasts likewise celebrated the BMW's smoothness, reliability, oil-tightness, and comfort. If one thinks about all those things which made the BMW reputation, then by implication he can sense what other motorcycles in the fifties and early sixties were like. No one ever complained that BMW's didn't have electric starters; one-kick starting was such a treat compared to most other machines.

Germans rather than the Japanese created civilized motorcycling. But most enthusiasts knew BMW's by reputation; the silent German twins bore premium pricetags which confined them to a small handful of enthusiasts. Only later did the Japanese sell to the many that which the Germans had reserved for the few.

9

*R60, equipped with an Earls-type front
suspension, came in two—and only two—
colors: black or white.*

Honda CB-77 Super Hawk

Hitting the electric starter button on a Honda CB-77 for the first time was a strange and foreign experience. Kickstarting had been the time-worn way to bring a motorcycle to life. Indeed, for many enthusiasts, the early Hondas were the first electric-start motorcycles ever seen. The starter would spin the engine over furiously, or so it seemed, until the vertical twin staggered into life. With two 24mm carburetors, sporty cam timing, and 10:1 pistons, a cold 305 needed generous choking; and when the single-overhead-cam engine lighted off, Super Hawk owners learned to warm them up. If this seemed a bit touchy to some riders, they could remind themselves that the 305cc Super Hawk was truly a high-performance piece of hardware.

The four-speed CB-77 would clear 100 mph in top, with the tachometer needle waving beyond 9,000 rpm. In the days when most 650's would struggle to break the century mark, when 7,500-rpm engines were "real screamers," when nothing under 500cc could be considered a man's machine, the Honda Super Hawk was a revelation.

Between old and new motorcycling, the Honda CB-77 formed a watershed. Modern motorcycles really arrived with the Super Hawk. It had amenities: dependable lights, full instrumentation, electric starting. It had performance: a highly efficient, powerful and compact engine; bulletproof reliability; full-width, double-leading-shoe brakes. The Super Hawk had civility: unbelievable smoothness (for 1961) and effective muffling.

There were other Japanese machines with similar features, but Honda had the best package. The CB-77 brought motorcycling into the modern age—and in so doing, captured America.

10

CB-77 has a basic honesty and economy of line—no frills. Its appearance isn't a product of a design studio.

Triumph Bonneville

Certain words in motorcycling interlock automatically. Triumph and Bonneville form one such combination. Bonneville was more than Triumph's label for its top-of-the-line 650 vertical twin. Triumph Bonneville spelled out a codeword in motorcycling; it signified style, power, handling, and reliability. Harley-Davidson's Sportsters had more power; Featherbed Nortons steered better; BMW's ran longer. But the Triumph Bonneville had a balance of handling, power, and reliability. And the Bonny had something more: class.

Triumph's line leader changed through the 1960's. The 1962 Bonneville and the 1968 version were basically the same motorcycle. Nevertheless, in the peculiar British system of refinement, the frame, brakes, and electrics all varied in the 1960's. Triumph experimented with engine bearings; compression ratios went up and down; camshaft timings moved around; and the engines changed in detail. But the heart of the Triumph Bonneville stayed constant: the long-stroke (71mm x 82mm) vertical twin breathed in through two 1$^3/_{16}$-inch Amal carburetors, developed about 50 horsepower at the engine sprocket, spun 6,500 rpm on a crankshaft without center main bearings, and galloped the bike well past 100 mph. The Bonneville was the best road-sports 650 in 1961, and it still was in 1969.

The bike's charisma had a solid foundation in the machine's integrity. Only at the close of the decade did the Bonny's charm begin to fade. Totally new motorcycles moved forward faster and faster. No matter how quickly slicked up, the Bonneville couldn't keep pace. Eventually, the bike's classic lines were smeared, and the name applied to a 750cc twin.

Born in the fifties and pensioned off in the seventies, the Triumph Bonneville had its halcyon days in the sixties.

Light, agile, and stable, the Bonneville had outstanding handling, yet the motorcycle could have sold on its appearance alone.

Suzuki 250 X-6

With its X-6, Suzuki redefined lightweight motorcycle performance in 1965. The Honda CB-72 Hawk had represented the Japanese approach to sporting lightweights—brisk but civil. Never a dazzling performer like the 305cc Super Hawk, the similar 250cc Hawk was obese. The twin-cylinder, single-overhead-cam CB-72 carried the extra burden of four-stroke weight. Yamaha's 250cc YDS2 could overwhelm a Honda Hawk, but the two-stroke twin owned a shocking record of unreliability. In the X-6, Suzuki created the modern lightweight road-sports motorcycle: a twin-cylinder, two-stroke machine with six-speed transmission, oil injection, and huge brakes.

Suzuki's two-stroke engine produced a lot of power from a little weight. And the X-6 proved reliable. Unlike Yamaha's YDS2, the 250cc Suzuki had alloy cylinders and pistons with carefully worked-out expansion rates. Piston seizures were uncommon. Moreover, the X-6 employed direct oil injection, and this new system not only metered oil to the engine precisely, but it also ended forever the bother of mixing two-stroke oil with gasoline.

Breathtaking acceleration characterized the X-6. With six speeds in the gearbox, Suzuki could tune a narrow, peaky powerband into the engine. The 250 two-stroke would rocket through the quarter-mile, snicking through one gear after another, and stopping the clocks in 15.3 seconds. That figure made the Suzuki a full second quicker than most other lightweights—and in the 250 class a second was a light-year. More important, the X-6 would continue to run hard without blowing itself into a bucket of shrapnel.

Power, reliability, and thoughtful amenities; those things made the Suzuki a legend in 1965. The high-performance road-sports two-stroke had truly arrived.

Ten years after its début, a good Hustler, vintage 1965, will trample its less powerful and heavier namesake of 1975.

Yamaha DT-1

With the DT-1, Yamaha created a new kind of motorcycle. In the middle and late 1960's, manufacturers tried to devise dual-purpose motorcycles, which could be ridden both on and off the road. Invariably, makers followed a simple expedient: they used street bikes, adding skid plates to protect the engine, raising exhaust pipes to increase ground clearance, and mounting knobby tires to complete the package. Dressing up a street machine in an off-road motif just didn't make a two-wheeler worthy for off-road travel. So Yamaha tried a fresh approach.

Pursuing the dual-purpose concept from another direction, Yamaha started by designing an off-road motorcycle which could be outfitted for street use. Such machines were not completely unknown. In Europe, for example, ISDT-type motorcycles were off-road competition mounts that carried minimal street gear. But Yamaha did not want to build anything so fine as a competition bike; they intended that the DT-1 be used for light-duty, off-road, pleasure riding. So it was important that the motorcycle have full street equipment and possess all the accoutrements of civil motorcycling.

Technology converged in the late 1960's to make the Yamaha innovation possible. Two-stroke engineering advances guaranteed that Yamaha could build a lightweight, single-cylinder two-stroke without long development time. Moreover, an oil injection system eliminated the chore of mixing oil in the gas; banishing this messy routine considerably broadened the DT-1's appeal.

The Yamaha approach to off-road pleasure bikes worked brilliantly. Suddenly all the street motorcycles-cum-trail bikes were overweight and outmoded. Motorcycle enthusiasts responded in large numbers to Yamaha's concept. They liked both the DT-1's off-road capability and its agility for round-town riding. Quickly, other Japanese companies rushed to produce their own "enduro" machines. But Yamaha remained the greatest beneficiary of that market first discovered and tapped by the DT-1.

Capped by a refrigerator-white gas tank,
the Yamaha hit a glory hole in the market.
Widespread off-road riding began with the DT-1.

Harley-Davidson Sportster

Harley-Davidson's Sportster reached its zenith in 1968. The year was a fitting time for its peak, since 1969 brought a whole new generation of big motorcycles. New Japanese machines made the Sportster look old; indeed, in a few short months in 1969, the famous Milwaukee V-twin aged a decade.

The giant 55-cubic-inch twin had a very basic appeal: appearance, sound, and straight-line performance. The Sportster belonged to the Romantic Age of motorcycling. Motorcycles were rugged mechanical devices which played to the senses. Bikes had no gadgets, no appliance-like character.

The Sportster projected an image of pure motorcycle. It was brutish and basic: two wheels were punctuated by an enormous V-twin engine. Nothing frilly; nothing pasted-on.

Romantics loved the V-twin's barking exhausts. The staggered firing impulses created a signature as distinctive as a fingerprint. The motorcycle seemed to bellow horsepower.

Straight-line performance did not belie the exhaust. The big-displacement V-twin could lever the 520-pound motorcycle through the standing-start quarter mile in 13.5 seconds. That white-knuckled acceleration, accompanied by full-throated exhaust din, gave the rider a trip full of sensations.

In an age when most big motorcycles leaked oil on garage floors, vibrated their riders, kickstarted with grim reluctance, snuffed out lightbulbs, and handled fast corners with uncertain malevolence, the Sportster was king. No one demanded motorcycles which were perfect appliances. Better that your big motorcycle said *mean-machine* than preserved a spotless garage floor. When it came to motorcycle imagery, nothing said *motorcycle* as well as Harley-Davidson's Sportster.

19

Many Harley owners personalize their bikes; but tank and pipes are classic sportster, individualized though the bike might be.

Kawasaki H1 500

The Kawasaki H1 was a gunshot motorcycle. Kawasaki intended that its 500cc, three-cylinder, two-stroke motorcycle, introduced in 1969, be quick and fast. More than that, the H1 proved absolutely hair-trigger sudden. American riders traditionally liked quick acceleration trips, and several modern Japanese two-strokes catered to the fast-departure crowd during the mid-1960's. Lightweights, such as the Suzuki X-6, were the crown princes of acceleration. The king of the drag strip was the H1. It played to the fast-exit instincts in every enthusiast.

Riders of the H1 specialized in impressive sprints between quarter-mile markers. Times dropped through the 13-second floor and into the high 12's. Terminal speeds in the quarter-mile traps hit 100 mph. The raw numbers became more impressive when one realized that full 750cc motorcycles could not match the Kawasaki 500's time-cards. Kawasaki demonstrated the kind of power which two-stroke engines could produce in full street trim. The Japanese company also showed the world the type of motorcycle which could result from such designs. Great horsepower and light running gear equaled a gunshot motorcycle.

No one praised the three-cylinder bike as a handler for good reasons. For openers, squeezing the throttle trigger sent the front wheel pawing in the air and on the one-two gearchange, the front tire would pop skyward again. If the Kawasaki exhibited an inclination to flying take-offs in a straight line, the bike had a dreadful reputation for wobbling and shaking when cornered with spirit; the over-zealous rider could bounce himself into a battered heap.

American enthusiasts soon grew out of their love affair with untamed rocketships. Having experienced straight-line super-performance, the American enthusiasts demanded something more than single-dimension motorcycles. Kawasaki, eager to please, gradually took the sting out of later H1 500's, and thus sent the original hot rod off to its place in history.

20

It didn't handle well, it wasn't very comfortable, and "quiet" was a word it didn't know, but the H1 sure was quick.

Honda CB-750 KO

Words poorly capture the importance of Honda's CB-750 KO. *Significant:* the first CB-750 redirected the path of motorcycle development; it blended shattering performance with appliance-like civility.

Innovative: the motorcycle reintroduced the four-cylinder engine to road-riding enthusiasts, carried the first genuinely workable hydraulic disc brake in the two-wheeled world, and offered a standard five-speed transmission in the 750 class. But the greatest innovation was the mass production of such an incredible machine.

Exciting: The Honda CB-750 KO gave the modern motorcyclist his first experience with a machine that quelled vibration, had dazzling engine performance (the standing quarter-mile passed in 13.4 seconds), impressive top speed (125 mph), outstanding brakes, remarkable handling—and an exhaust note which mesmerized.

Had the CB-750 been able to perform well in two or three categories, it would have been a memorable machine. But the CB-750 KO had top-rank credentials in almost every measure. For pure excitement, nothing in 1969 could equal the Honda 750.

The years have blunted the impact of Honda's 750. It proved such a pivotal machine that other manufacturers followed the lead established by Honda. As the CB-750 gathered company from other makers, Honda's glory-bike lost its uniqueness. Moreover, by further refining and civilizing later editions of the CB-750, Honda managed to dull the sharp edge of the original 750. Subsequent standard versions never matched the engine performance of that first magnificent Honda 750.

Honda's innovation extended beyond a mass-produced four-cylinder bike; the 750 was first with a hydraulic disc brake.

Roadburners

Motorcycling grew up on roads, and as roadways changed, motorcycles adapted. Very early motorcycles in the United States were light and spindly. When rain dissolved dusty roads into mucky bogs, a pioneer motorcyclist could at least drag his mount through the pasty mud. Later, the hardtop roads of the twenties and thirties allowed American motorcycles to become larger and heavier. Thanks to hard-surfacing, the motorcyclist no longer had to portage his machine after a downpour.

Today roads still subtly shape motorcycles. Roadburners are the most powerful, sophisticated, and expensive machines available to the general motorcycling public. All these heavy, pavement-bound vehicles can gobble up mile after mile.

The term "roadburner" reaches across a broad spectrum. At one pole there are long-distance touring machines. They transport riders (and passengers) in great luxury; their domain is broad highways with gentle curves. Touring is wide-eyed motorcycling. The journey—what is seen, and done, and sensed along the way—is the thing; both the motorcycle and the road are tools for this larger experience.

Other roadburners form the spectrum's center. Grand-touring motorcycles can cover long distances at high average speeds over roads both straight and winding. Such machines must handle as precisely on twisting asphalt as on wide, concrete interstates. Strong engines and stout brakes are requisite. Road holding can't be sacrificed for luxurious comfort, yet the grand touring machine must not exhaust the rider.

At the spectrum's far end, pure sporting roadsters—including café racers—provide high intensity/short duration motorcycling. The primary consideration is the machine's ability to hurtle along straight or snaky roads at terrific speeds. Comfort counts for little. Luxury means nothing; stark function is everything. The gods are power, handling, and braking. There's no wide-screen journey; the total experience takes place between the road, machine, and rider.

The only thing that roadburners share is the road itself. A touring bike and a café racer are quite different motorcycling experiences.

Honda GL-1000

The Gold Wing Honda is a two-wheeler with a four-wheeled soul. The GL-1000 surely must be the most automotive motorcycle ever produced. The water-cooled, 1-litre boxer engine does not shout out *motorcycle;* massive and complex, the aluminum giant goes about its business with quiet, unruffled efficiency. The engine never calls attention to itself. Hidden inside its water-jacketing, the engine seems compartmentalized. It's just as remote from the rider as a luxury car's engine is distant from the steering wheel. The rider meets the powerful four-cylinder only at the controls and instrument facia.

Smoothness, silence, and weight count heavily in any luxury rating, and the Honda GL-1000 scores easily. This magnificent touring con-

veyance is the smoothest-running motorcycle in the world. Vibration won't fatigue the rider; nor will the ripples and pocks of interstate highways numb the senses and pound the body. The Gold Wing insulates the rider from every harshness of motorcycling.

Luxury often means weight, and at 650 pounds, the GL-1000 is a lot of motorcycle. The Honda has a heavy drive shaft in order to eliminate the inconveniences of chain drive. Honda also employs a counter-rotating balancer to cancel out almost all the torque reaction long associated with boxer engines.

The generous proportions and ample size of the GL-1000 give the rider an opportunity to carry all necessary luggage—and still leave room for a passenger. And if there's anything better than a time and space machine for one, it's such a device for two.

Built expressly for long-distance touring,
the giant Honda, with its water-cooled, opposed
engine, looks like nothing else.

The instrument pod's face-cover opens when the ignition key is switched on. No bike has more warning lights than the RE5.

Suzuki RE5 Rotary

Motorcyclists are tradition-bound creatures, perhaps because motorcycles only slowly escape time-locked conventions. Truly revolutionary motorcycles are difficult to create; after all, the ways of packaging an engine into an effective two-wheeled vehicle are limited. In the past decade, engines have made the most remarkable advances with the proliferation of two- and four-stroke multis, and the emergence of modern V-twins. Suzuki carried powerplant innovation outside the mainstream with the début of their Wankel-system, rotary-engined motorcycle.

The RE5 is strikingly novel. At first the engine bay looks shockingly alien; the lines of the single-rotor, water-cooled Wankel form an unfamiliar pattern. Soon one's eye picks out some standard components—carburetor, ignition-breaker blister, oil filter—in new places.

At idle the RE5 sounds neither like a four-stroke nor two-stroke **28** engine, but something in between. On the road, with the exhaust noise

drumming out the dual mufflers, the rider can enjoy the machine's nearly total absence of vibration. The most unforgettable characteristic is the almost hydraulic quality of the RE's power. It's quite unlike the quality of power produced by standard reciprocating engines, which, no matter how smooth and sub-divided into small cylinders, still deliver power with an impulse-character.

Suzuki's rotary qualifies as the most complex engine ever to power a standard production motorcycle. The lubrication, ignition, and carburetion systems perform far more intricate tasks than their counterparts in reciprocating engines. Furthermore, construction tolerances are considerably more precise and tighter than in conventional engines. The rotary engine is no place for shady-tree mechanics to stage exploratory operations.

The Suzuki probably will not create a rotary-engine revolution. But most new motorcycles soon find their advocates inside the sport; so if nothing else, Suzuki's masterful engineering exercise will allow motorcycling to develop its first real rotary partisans.

MV Agusta 750S America

Two camshafts, four cylinders, a five-speed gearbox, and a six-thousand-dollar pricetag—the MV Agusta 750S America carries an impressive set of numbers. The 750's pedigree traces directly back to the company's grand prix road racers; faithful to racing practices, MV lavishes time and resources on the construction of the motorcycle. Some other roadburners have double overhead camshaft engines, but the valves are driven by chains. The 788cc engine, however, as a derivative of a racing engine, runs the camshafts more precisely with a drive-train of spur-cut gears. It's outrageously expensive, yet that's the way MV Agusta does things.

Both compact and massive, the 750 America belies its 560-pound wet weight. The engine cases are actually narrower than those of the Honda CB-400 Four. Inside the Italian engine vault spins a vast assortment of gears. An electric starter snaps the engine to life, and a great thrash rises from the cylinderhead, wherein the valve train operates. The exhaust note, barely modulated by four megaphone-shaped mufflers, overwhelms all space surrounding the motorcycle. Others might call it racket; motorcyclists (and the MV factory) insist it's pure music.

On the road the 750S sheds its bulky feeling. The motorcycle meets the rider at every juncture of the senses. The hand- and foot-controls have finely honed movements; the fabulous close-ratio gearbox shifts with the best lever-action in motorcycling.

Fast, expensive, and exclusive, 750S America models are built slowly, by hand, one by one. At the outside 200 machines will reach American shores each year. So most enthusiasts will meet the 750S in the library of last refuge: a perfect daydream trimmed in sound and speed.

The 788cc engine pulls strongly from 2,000 rpm to 9,000 rpm. Power reaches the rear wheel via a drive shaft.

Suzuki GT-750 LeMans

Before the introduction of Suzuki's liquid-cooled GT-750 LeMans, radiators were devices only for exotic road-racing motorcycles. Common production two-strokes made do with air cooling. Indeed, one virtue of two-stroke engines, as their adherents fondly pointed out, was basic simplicity. But stone-axe two-stroke engineering ended in the mid-1960's with direct oil injection and seizure-resistant pistons and cylinder liners.

Suzuki's LeMans represents the current culmination of two-stroke technology as applied to a basic touring motorcycle. Heart of this long-distance runner is a liquid-cooled, three-cylinder, two-stroke engine. The cooling system permits the Suzuki to maintain very close running tolerances, reduce engine noise, lower gasoline consumption, and raise engine efficiency.

Suzuki has tuned the GT-750 engine with the touring rider in mind. The triple will slog forward with tractor-like willingness with the tachometer waving in its lower reaches. The power continues, sharply building toward its peak at 7,000 rpm. Its strong engine enables the GT-750 to haul big loads, including a sidecar. There's no worrying when pulling up a grade, because the liquid-cooled engine stays even-temperatured and tireless. Downhill, the outstanding double-disc brake provides stop-action halts if necessary. Otherwise, the superb brake offers an extra measure of security to those riders who pack heavy loads.

The 550-pound bike earns few honors as a backroad demon-racer. But the rider—proceeding at a normal rate—will stay comfortable in the generous saddle, cushioned by the soft suspension which intercepts and smothers bumps along the way. The miles roll under the liquid-cooled Suzuki and disappear effortlessly over a receding horizon.

So the GT-750 has a peculiar kind of sorcery: an enthusiast settles behind the bars and he begins at once to think of places far distant.

Water cooling gives the GT-750 a distinctive, almost startling, appearance. The bike meets every test for a long-distance runner.

Moto Guzzi Sport

The Moto Guzzi Sport holds the middle ground. The machine fits perfectly into the grand touring category, exactly halfway between luxurious touring motorcycles (like the Suzuki GT-750) and pure sporting mounts (such as the Ducati 750 Desmo).

Moto Guzzi owners contend that their machines have achieved the perfect compromise. The Italian V-twin can cope with winding roads far better than straight tourers. Like touring bikes, the Guzzi remains comfortable for long hauls. Moreover, the shaft-driven Latin has a good record for reliability and fiddle-free maintenance. The Guzzi's long-distance capabilities separate it from café racers and most other super-performance bikes. Certainly the Guzzi Sport lacks the tautness in cornering and the raw horsepower of pure sporting roadsters, yet this V-twin can't be outclassed on a winding road unless the company is motoring very hard indeed.

The Italian twin has excellent all-round performance; in that respect, the Italian bike resembles the Kawasaki Z-1. The Sport handles better than the 903, but lacks the refinement and immense horsepower of the dazzling Japanese twin-cam four.

Guzzi's 90-degree pushrod twin has developed from an original 700cc to a present 750cc. The stablemate of the 750cc Sport, the 850-T, is intended for touring only. Despite its small engine, the Guzzi Sport has not been booted out of the high-performance club and relegated to the minor leagues.

There will always be a Guzzi in the roadburner class—the **34** company's experience and Italian preferences guarantee it.

Graceful and flowing, the original Sport
(with drum brake instead of discs) is more handsome
than later models with contrived styling.

Triumph Trident 750

The Trident, though the flagship of the Triumph line, lurked for years in the shadow of the Triumph 650/750 vertical twin. So strong and pervasive was the influence of the twin, the three-cylinder superbike only achieved full recognition after the reorganized company dropped production of the popular vertical twin.

Hard economic facts explained the triple's survival and the twin's demise. The three-cylinder model could be profitably developed and further refined. The old twin had simply reached its final stage, and had no real future.

Though first released in 1969, and face-lifted shortly thereafter, the **36** Triumph Trident continued fundamentally unchanged until 1975. A

five-speed transmission proved to be the best addition to the motorcycle in its first five years.

In 1975 the Trident underwent a dramatic overhaul. The basic silhouette of the machine changed. The all-new Trident picked up a stripped profile similar to the BSA Rocket Three, the Trident's original stablemate, which was dropped in 1972. The forward cant of the new Trident engine, à la the Rocket Three, permitted Triumph to incorporate an electric starter. A new rear disc brake complemented the disc stopper up front.

Fresh, bold styling gave the new Trident a kind of jaunty confidence which the old bike always lacked. The three-cylinder roadster may finally receive its due. Insiders always knew the old triple was an excellent motorcycle. Now, in its revitalized form, everyone will know. **37**

Left-side shifting, as required by United States federal standards, has been incorporated in the stylish new Trident.

BMW R90S

Leader of the BMW line, the R90S is the most expensive motorcycle generally available. Only limited-edition motorcycles (Laverda 1000, Ducati 750 Desmo, and MV Agusta 750SS) are more costly. BMW enthusiasts accept the hefty $3,800 pricetag for a Teutonic version of substance, luxury, and performance.

The R90S delivers. The machine bespeaks substance everywhere. The engine castings are ruggedly handsome; the paint, flawless. BMW chrome has a deep luster, the result of careful polishing, precise application, and thorough buffing. Attention to detail makes the R90S the best-finished motorcycle in the world.

The workmanship so evident in BMW construction finds a match in its luxury on the highway. Beyond the normal complement of instruments, the R90S's facia (inside the fairing) contains an electric clock. There's no ungentlemanly chain; a virtually maintenance-free shaft drive carries power to the rear wheel. The long-stroke front suspension devours all bumps before the disturbances reach the rider or passenger. BMW has tuned the suspension to maximize comfort; though high-speed handling suffers a bit, only hard-riding devotees of twisting roads would fault BMW's calibration.

The engine's silence and smoothness belie its performance. The horizontally opposed twin breathes through monster 38mm carburetors, easily spins to 7,200 rpm, and drives nearly 500 pounds of motorcycle beyond 120 mph. The R90S hardly dawdles up its acceleration curve. From a standstill, 100 mph comes up in less than 13 seconds. Yet the most impressive part of R90S performance is its tremendous torque; even in top gear, cracking the throttle open produces an astonishing surge forward.

No wonder BMW enthusiasts insist that $4,000 still buys a lot in today's world.

*Eight inches of front fork travel keep
bumps away from the rider; at highway speeds,
the twin runs with mellow smoothness.*

Norton 850 John Player Special

The Norton 850 John Player Special runs in the shadow of a long tradition. The engine's lineage can be traced directly back to the late 1940's. Today, big-displacement vertical twins are out of fashion in a motorcycle world filled with triples and fours. No one save Norton still makes engine and gearbox separate. With four speeds, the Norton has one fewer than the norm of the seventies.

Yet the Norton has grown old with style and grace. The motorcycle's brilliant Isolastic system mounts the engine, gearbox, and swinging arm in a sub-frame. Thanks to rubber bushings between the sub-frame and main structure, the terrific vibrations from the big twin are isolated from the rider. Though it judders below 2,500 rpm, the bike becomes remarkably smooth above that engine speed.

If its engineering is dated, the Norton still does not want for style. The standard Commando Roadster and Commando Interstate are two of the

best-looking motorcycles anywhere. The new John Player Special is named after Norton's factory road-racing bikes which are sponsored by the John Player Tobacco Company. Quick to pick up on new styling trends, Norton has rendered the JPS in café-racer idiom.

Café racers, which mock road-racing bikes, set comfort and convenience aside so that form may follow function everywhere. What's the function? Fast riding on winding roads! A good café racer should have substantial power, excellent brakes, first-line tires and suspension, and lightweight running stock. Other race-track trappings may include large gas tanks, solo saddles, clip-on bars, and fairings.

The Player Norton meets these tests: 48 horsepower at the rear wheel, 475 pounds wet, Lockheed front disc brake, solid British handling, great Dunlop TT100 tires, gas tank shroud, solo seat, clip-ons, and three-quarters fairing. The dual headlamps add a distinctive touch.

Old the Norton may be, but this speedy veteran certainly comes dressed in elegant, modish fashions. **41**

*Norton's 850cc vertical twin
has been buried by a three-quarters
fairing and a full-tank cowling.*

Kawasaki Z-1

When Kawasaki introduced the Z-1 late in 1972, the motorcycle caused a sensation. It represented the state of Japanese art in high-performance sporting roadsters. The passing years have not dulled its appeal.

The engine is simply magnificent. The 903cc unit has chain-driven, double overhead camshafts, four 28mm carburetors, a mild 8.5:1 compression ratio, a robust roller-bearing crankshaft, and a 9,000-rpm redline. The Z-1 engine has an excellent record for reliability—and an awesome reputation for power. It's well deserved: the Kawasaki produces a genuine 80-plus horsepower at the rear wheel.

More than anything else, the engine makes the Z-1 what it is. The twin-cam, four-cylinder powerplant will send the Kawasaki heavyweight through the standing quarter-mile inside 12.4 seconds. No other roadburner can whip a good Z-1 on the drag strip. And the 903cc motorcycle has a top speed well beyond 130 mph, and that figure

Though the Z-1 does many things well,
the most important part of the motorcycle is its
super-power 903cc twin-cam engine.

guarantees that few street-going vehicles will humiliate a Z-1, police cars excepted!

To dwell on brute performance does the Kawasaki an injustice. It does many things very well. Despite its 540-pound weight, the Z-1's disc brake can quickly erase speed, and the bike steers surprisingly well. The engine runs smoothly, without a trace of evil temperament. The Kawasaki, like any other refined, civil Japanese motorcycle, blurbles into life at the touch of its starter button. The bike possesses all those features for rider convenience, from indicator-warning lights to helmet holders.

Under 5,000 rpm, one might mistake the Z-1 for just another well-engineered-and-executed Japanese motorcycle—nice for short trips, pleasant on winding roads, and enjoyable on long interstate treks. But above 5,000 rpm, with the giant engine howling toward its 9,000-rpm bloodline, no rider will ever forget he's aboard motorcycledom's quickest and fastest production roadster.

Laverda 1000

Despite all the trappings of refinement and civility, the beast, aggressive and strong, still roars inside some motorcycles. The Italian Laverda 1000 makes the point perfectly. Consider a few of the motorcycle's credentials for civility: lovely Nippon Seiki instruments (not Italian-issue pointers); Japanese hand-switch controls (the world's best); Bosch electrical components (complete with pointless ignition). These items might suggest a plush touring machine, Italian/International style.

What a shock the real Laverda 1000 would be! The double overhead camshaft engine dominates the motorcycle. Physically, the bike seems small, for the saddle is low and the engine massive. The claim of 80 horsepower can be no sly puffery; the 520-pound motorcycle has tremendous acceleration. Yet its surge lacks spiteful suddenness. The three-cylinder engine has such wide power (from idle-to-8,000 rpm) that the bike launches forward with velvet quickness.

Laverda contains its monster engine inside a stout and rigid frame. The first-class suspension components and the frame make the Laverda a memorable roadholder on winding roads. Laverda has set up the suspension for fast work on twisting venues, and in such places the huge Italian multi can proceed with fantastic swiftness.

The beast does not love underachievers. The clutch lever demands a strong hand; so does the twistgrip. Around town the Laverda feels bulky and heavy. The stiff suspension will punish the timid soul with a harsh ride at slow speeds. After ten minutes in the saddle, a jarred novice would conclude the 1000 was something less than its civil appearance promised. Only an expert motorcyclist would want this one-litre lion. And only an expert could appreciate its excellence.

44

Extraordinarily narrow, the engine squeezes into a very small space; yet it still overwhelms the bike.

Ducati 750 Desmo Super Sport

Building a new V-twin hardly seemed progressive in the early 1970's. The mainstream of modern motorcycle design all flowed toward in-line transverse multi-cylinder engines. Multis became popular because these engines were both smooth and powerful. True, three- and four-cylinder engines were often wide and heavy, but silky power outweighed all other considerations. Nevertheless, Ducati built a V-twin.

The Italian 90-degree V-twin has perfect primary balance; consequently Ducati 750 engines—in touring or sports versions—are all but vibration-free. Easily the smoothest twin in the world, the Ducati 750 is even more placid than the 750 Honda or 900 Kawasaki four-cylinder bikes. Mounted longitudinally, the Ducati unit has no periodic quaking like Moto Guzzi's twin or BMW's boxer engine.

Though its layout requires a long wheelbase (61 inches), the Ducati can be much narrower and considerably lighter than a multi of equal displacement. The Ducati Super Sport weighs just over 450 pounds. That makes the 750 twin lighter than a 550cc Suzuki two-stroke!

No twin can outpower a similarly-tuned multi of equal size. Yet Ducati's GT-750 (a grand-touring bike) and the 750 Sport (a café-racer model) give little horsepower away to multis. The 750 Super Sport, with desmodromic valve actuation (valves are both opened and closed mechanically), can outgun other sporting bikes. Ducati engines may make slightly less horsepower than equivalent multis, but they still perform brilliantly, thanks to a favorable power-to-weight ratio.

Other features beyond its power-to-weight ratio and valve system mark the 750 SS as a pure sporting motorcycle. Nothing can touch the Ducati for handling; its fantastic stability and sureness around corners makes it the fastest-cornering production machine available.

Ducatis have few ''convenience'' features. Finishing and detailing rate fair-to-poor for expensive motorcycles. As a well-rounded motorcycle for the everyday enthusiast, the Ducati 750 SS is a disaster. As **46** a pure sporting motorcycle, it's a masterpiece.

Desmo is a lean and Spartan motorcycle.
The engine will rev beyond 9,000 rpm, where
it roars with blood-boiling ferocity.

Honda CB-750 Super Sport

Face lifting, a Detroit concept, has its practitioners in the motorcycle world. Reckless metal-surgery can be dangerous. Should inspiration fail, a golden coach can be transformed into a yellow pumpkin. Nothing in motorcycling has been such a golden carriage as Honda's CB-750; understandably Honda has never radically altered the bike. After all, the CB-750 has had the widest buyer appeal of any roadburner. Consequently, like the standard 750, Honda built its new CB-750 Super Sport for the broadest possible audience.

The Super Sport Honda supplements, but does not supersede, the familiar standard version of the 750 Honda. The sporty 750 offers subdued, almost compromised, café-racer styling. Undiluted café racers are monoposto machines; but the Honda Super Sport, like the BMW R90S, has a two-up seat with tail section. By Honda standards, a mono-saddle would have seriously diminished the bike's appeal. And while the sporting set might have raved over low bars, most customers would likely opt for higher, more comfortable bars. Hence, the Super Sport has high bars.

Yet the go-fasters have not been entirely ignored. Hard riders will welcome the new rear-wheel disc brake. The Super Sport also features a four-into-one exhaust system which is lighter than the standard 750 four-muffler plumbing. The Super Sport's single silencer throttles the exhaust to a whisper-level without suffocating engine performance.

Clever touches abound. The Super Sport has a recessed gas cap, hidden from view by a key-lock door. And the ignition-key/fork-lock switch between the instruments allows the rider to turn off the engine and lock the front fork in one motion.

Despite the face lift, and all the new equipment, the best thing about the Super Sport is something "old": the basic 750 Honda engine—stronger than ever and still smooth and reliable.

The Super Sport, with far more power
than the standard 750 Honda, remains stable and
predictable approaching its cornering limit.

•3
Sporting Middleweights

Efficiency has always been a password in motorcycling. Modern engine technology has enabled manufacturers to squeeze increasing power from engines of given displacements. Two-stroke engines best illustrate this high-efficiency engineering, for a contemporary two-stroke can produce a staggering amount of power for its displacement, size, and weight.

Among the principal beneficiaries of this efficiency-technology have been mid-displacement sporting roadsters. These 350cc-550cc motorcycles carry powerful, compact engines in good handling chassis. In almost every case the go-power of the engines is equaled by the stopping authority of disc brakes.

Only select middle-displacement motorcycles can qualify as sporting mounts. Other machines of similar size belong to a commuter-class of vehicle. Compared to the sporting roadsters, the commuters are dull, bland transporters, which seem soft and lethargic. The mid-sized sportsters feel lean, taut, and vital.

The sporting middleweights perform best on roads which chase over the countryside in a series of zigzags. The engines provide lively acceleration for the nimble bikes that can slice through corners deftly. The motorcycles feel so energetic; they respond instantaneously to rider inputs. If the rider twitches in the saddle, the bike moves.

Motorcyclists love the sporting middleweights because the bikes are such willing performers. The enthusiast can sense the bike is trying hard, matching him move for move. Going quickly, a union develops between man and metal. Howling out of a corner, with the tach needle waving at the redline and a footpeg skimming the ground, the motorcyclist is one with his machine and the road below.

Midweights, which carry "big" engines in compact packages, have an outstanding balance of power, brakes, and handling.

Yamaha RD-350

The RD-350 Yamaha is a pure sporting motorcycle: phenomenal acceleration, first-class handling, and incredible braking. A well-tuned 350cc Yamaha twin can give many 650's and 750's a fit in a straight-line dash; and on snaky roads, the powerful, nimble Yamaha can out-scoot anything, save a small number of sporting roadburners. With 34 horsepower at the rear wheel, the 350-pound two-stroke rockets through a standing quarter-mile in 14.1 seconds. Geared for acceleration rather than a high top speed, the RD-350 will just miss 100 mph full chat in top (sixth) gear.

Docile and mild-mannered the Yamaha isn't. Below 4,000 rpm, the two-stroke engine spits out a syncopated tune through its mufflers. Then at 4,000 rpm—where it moves into its tuned powerband—the engine really chimes in. In several short-coupled instants, the tachometer needle sweeps to 8,000 rpm. The rider automatically firms up his grip at the bars because the front end aviates in the lower gears.

The suspension is taut as a hard-drawn string in perfect tune. The RD-350 offers no cushy perch; the rider gets quick, accurate handling, and a confident sense of stability when heeled over in a corner.

Like any fast, snappish motorcycle, the Yamaha twin brooks no fools. Erratic, ham-fisted cowboys will unseat themselves on the potent two-stroke. The acceleration which the seven-port, reed-valve twin can generate and the deceleration that the disc brake can provide (beyond one G!) marks the RD-350 as a high-intensity, full-attention vehicle. So excellent is the Yamaha as a sporting device, only riders with skill and finesse can fully master this brilliant machine.

53

*Parked silently at roadside,
the Yamaha RD-350 cools off after lacing up
a tortuous mountain road.*

Kawasaki 400 S-3

Kawasaki built its American empire on performance motorcycles. Enthusiasts are not likely to forget the first-generation 500cc and 750cc Kawasaki three-cylinder two-strokes, which had absolutely boggling straight-line acceleration. But these noisy, vibrating, gas-guzzling two-strokes aged gracelessly. They were to be experienced, and then sold.

The 903 Z-1 Kawasaki lifted the mantle of super-performance from the H2. Meanwhile, though Kawasaki detuned the 500cc triple, the company never succeeded in making the H1 a well-balanced sporting roadster. Filling that slot was the Kawasaki S-3 400cc two-stroke triple, a motorcycle which had grown out of a smaller 350cc version.

Enjoying the blessings of a strong, willing engine, the 400cc Kawasaki offers vivid acceleration. That's in keeping with Kawasaki

Sporting midweights, like the S-3, carry full instrumentation; Kawasaki-style two-stroke power makes the 400 very quick.

heritage. Indeed, only the 350 Yamaha twin can best the triple through the standing quarter-mile.

With the muscular engine comes a peaky power curve. The 400 feels uninspired until the tachometer needle has covered the first 4,500 rpm; after that point, forward progress becomes quite rapid.

The disc brake up front will yank the S-3 Kawasaki to a halt should exigencies demand clamping down hard on the brake lever. Yet sporting roadsters encourage their riders to be smooth. Like other fast middleweights, the Kawasaki triple is basically agile and stable, but limited shock-absorber damping lets the triple rock on its suspension when cornering hard. Bump-strewn corners will require the Kawasaki rider to click down his pace; otherwise, he and his two-stroke triple can happily lace their way along a back-country road.

Suzuki GT-380 Sebring

Suzuki pioneered the six-speed gearbox in modern lightweight production motorcycles. Its 250cc X-6, introduced in 1965, first underscored the advantages of six-speed gearboxes. Today, six-speed transmissions are becoming the rule in 350cc–400cc road/sports bikes. The Suzuki 380 Sebring, the Honda CB-400 Super Sport, and the Yamaha RD-350 all go forward with six speeds; only the Kawasaki 400cc triple lacks the number-six cog.

Traditionally manufacturers have used six-speed transmissions in conjunction with peaky engines that are tuned for maximum horsepower in a narrow, elevated powerband. Here the GT-380 Suzuki presents a surprise. The three-cylinder, two-stroke engine has been engineered for a very wide spread of power. Willing to pull with determination from 3,000 rpm, the power characteristics pose a question: why should Suzuki bother with both a broad powerband and an elaborate transmission?

Suzuki has designed the six-speed transmission as a substitute for more horsepower. The transmission permits the Sebring to make maximum use of its mildly tuned engine. Since the 30-horsepower GT-380 outweighs all its 350/400 counterparts, the six-speed gearbox reduces the practical effect of the Suzuki's inferior power-to-weight ratio.

Much of the Sebring's weight relates to its size and luxury. Physically the GT-380 is built on a larger scale than other 350/400cc motorcycles. For example, the Suzuki 380 has a wheelbase 3 inches longer than Yamaha's RD-350 (52 vs. 55 inches).

The six-speed gearbox coupled to the mild-mannered engine gives the cyclist a wide choice in his riding. If he wishes to cruise pleasantly at a low hum, the engine will lug along happily. On the other hand, the rider may make full use of the six-speed transmission, summon the engine to its strongest high-rpm range, rely on the GT-380's first-string handling and braking, and flail away on roads that dart and swing through the countryside.

56

The Suzuki GT-380's exhaust plumbing is tucked up and in nicely; the pipes won't contact the ground during spirited riding.

Honda CB-400 Super Sport

Some motorcycles have a watch-like quality, and Honda's CB-400 Super Sport radiates the same *machine-ness* as an intricate watch with jeweled movements. Perhaps one could believe that Honda designed and built the 350/400 series just as a technical exercise—to demonstrate that Honda could produce such a small four-cylinder machine. But more likely Honda believed that an audience existed for a watch-like motorcycle. It did.

The Super Sport is an updated version of the CB-350 Four. The 1975 face-lift gave the bike its trim café-racer looks, pushed the engine displacement to 408cc's, and put a number-six gear in the transmission.

Everywhere the little four-cylinder machine gives the rider a sense of substance. The solid powerplant will rev to its 10,000-rpm redline with muted fury, thanks to the four-into-one exhaust system. Lots of revs, little noise—this combination gives the rider a solid feeling about the bike. The Honda never does anything unexpected and displays no cammy, high-strung nature. The engine seems content to hum docilely at 4,000 rpm, but an energetic rider has the six-speed gearbox to keep the engine boiling near its redline for maximum performance. The Super Sport will mirror the inclination of the rider. The Yamaha RD-350 encourages full-blooded riding at all times. The Honda makes no demands whatever on its rider.

The CB-400's soft suspension lets the bike hobby-horse a bit as cornering speeds increase, but the rocking doesn't undercut the basic feeling of security. Gentle bobbing won't discourage hot passages in following corners. Breakneck schedules aside, the bike has a full-enjoyment speed on highways which thread through the hills; a quick and lively pace permits the rider to hear the engine notes rise and fall, and to sense the mechanism of a very enchanting watch.

*The CB-400 has a liquid kind of power
ample to 7,000, and strong to 10,000, rpm.
The Honda Four can really fly.*

Suzuki GT-550 Indy

Suzuki GT-550: the GT prefix stands for Grand Touring, and the Indy 550 fits the class perfectly. The 550cc three-cylinder two-stroke hasn't the brute power of heavy-caliber grand-touring machines, such as the Guzzi Sport or Kawasaki Z-1, but the Suzuki's silence, luxury, road holding, and braking mark the bike as a true GT mount.

The fierceness displayed by the Yamaha RD-350 does not infect the Suzuki triple. Indeed, the Indy produces less horsepower than the Yamaha 350—and the Suzuki's extra weight (100 pounds) takes the hard sting out of GT-550's straight-line performance. Nonetheless, the Indy quickly responds to throttle inputs; the engine pulls with determi-

nation from the lower portions of its rpm range. There's no waiting for

Though it looks like an enlarged Suzuki GT-380, the 550 Indy is a completely separate bike—larger and more powerful.

4,000 rpm to build up on the clock before the scenery begins to flash past. The Indy feels decidedly more brisk than Honda's four-stroke CB-550, which replies more softly to low-rpm throttle openings.

The briskness and precision with which the Suzuki moves makes the bike a pleasure. Exploiting the 550's exceptional handling, the enthusiastic rider can arc along a winding road without slit-eyed concentration. Sufficient power is available through the rev range, so the rider never feels that he's working hard—or flogging the bike.

Its evenness explains the Indy's success. So marvelously balanced and civilized, yet so responsive to its rider, the half-litre Suzuki can wheel along—swiftly, safely, effortlessly—without producing a chain of harried moments.

Honda CB-550

Some machines have a natural harmony, and the Honda CB-550 is one such machine. Perhaps more by happy accident than willful design, all the individual elements of some motorcycles converge in perfect rhythm. The frame and running gear, using a factory's standard-formula calculations, work astoundingly well in particular cases. The power-plant, again built according to the constructor's handbook, emerges far better than logic might suggest.

Consider the Honda CB-550 Four. That this unit is smoother than Honda's larger 750 Four would come as no surprise. That's exactly what one might guess given the 550's smaller and lighter reciprocating parts. Then consider that the CB-550 runs more smoothly and easily than the Honda 350/400 Four series. That's unexpected. What explains the **62** unlikely difference? Doubtless the answers are hidden in many small

engineering numbers, but most riders instinctively feel the answer when they try a CB-550. The entire machine is a case of natural harmony.

The intermediate four-cylinder bike resists hard categorization. Thousands of 550's have toured the United States in every direction. For the suburban rider who likes to hop around town, the 550 whisks through traffic, never raising a disturbance.

Honda's half-litre bike has a sporting nature. The 10,000-rpm four-banger yowling in anger toward its limit is enough to excite most enthusiasts. The basic running stock isn't overtaxed by the engine's output, and that's a snag which mars many larger Japanese machines. Performance-minded riders favor the CB-550, which can be tweaked reliably for more horsepower and better handling.

When someone asks why Honda has been so successful in motorcycling, he shouldn't search for the answer in advertising copy or television commercials. He need only ride a CB-550. **63**

*Honda's 550 has a velvet smoothness
to it; even when rushing along at a pretty fair
rate, the bike never feels pressed.*

Enduro motorcycles try to serve two competing masters: motor vehicle regulations and the requirements of rough-terrain riding. Dual-purpose bikes, designed for street and trail riding, must carry full street equipment for legal operation on public thoroughfares. Unfortunately, headlamps, directional signals, and other street hardware become unwanted—and easily damaged—baggage in off-road riding areas.

Most manufacturers engineer their enduro bikes for only occasional, casual use off-road. Street/trail machines meet the demands of motor vehicle departments far better than the exigencies of off-road riding. That's understandable because a stunning majority of dual-purpose motorcycles never venture from the highways.

Other enduro motorcycles have been seriously designed for off-road action. Generally, these machines have only rudimentary electrical systems to meet the thin letter of the law. That suits dedicated out-back riders who would not waste an excellent off-road motorcycle on the street.

Enduro motorcycles are very personal tools. Riding off-road, an enthusiast can run harder and exploit his machine far more than his pavement-bound brethren on full street motorcycles. Consequently, the off-road rider soon knows his motorcycle intimately and discovers quickly his personal preferences in machinery. With experience his awareness expands: steering geometry, suspension action, riding positions, power characteristics, etc.

Dedicated off-road riders modify their motorcycles to individual riding tastes. One enthusiast may recast a Japanese dual-purpose bike as a way to create his ''perfect enduro.'' Another rider may tailor an already-specialized European mount. In all cases, solid starting points are necessary, and the following machines represent the finest points of departure generally available.

The off-road pilot can concentrate on riding his motorcycle and developing his communication with it—in an auto-free environment.

Montesa V75 Enduro

Typical of first-rate enduro motorcycles in the European style, the Montesa V75 Enduro exhibits a rugged and effective simplicity. Spartan in appearance, the single-cylinder Spanish two-stroke merely has token hardware for street riding. Like the German Maico and Austro-American Penton, the Montesa V75 is almost a motocross bike recalibrated to enduro specifications.

Handling and power characteristics identify the Montesa as an expert's off-road machine. The engine has little low-rpm torque and much high-rpm horsepower. Consequently, the Montesa rider can't plug along slowly with his mount. So it's a good thing that the V75's off-road handling improves as the pace over rough terrain gets hotter.

The Spanish bike employs a cantilever rear suspension system. The extra-long shock absorbers connect to the swinging arm at the conventional junctures. But then the dampers tilt forward at 45 degrees to join the frame at points far forward and lower than standard designs. Such a layout permits an increased up-and-down travel of the rear wheel. In theory, additional rear-wheel travel can result in greater rider comfort and better bump-control and directional stability in the rough.

As a lean, hard, enduro bike, the Montesa is built without frills. Riders must mix gas and oil for fuel since the V75 does not have two-stroke oil injection. The trim 260-pound motorcycle has no place for things such as directional signals.

Yet clever ideas often accompany starkness. Consider the Montesa's gasoline valves. Rather than using the familiar aluminum petcocks, the Montesa has a rubber bladder with a moveable steel ball which regulates (on-off-reserve) fuel flow. It's light, simple, and functional. Just like the rest of the V75 Enduro.

Montesa's cantilever rear
suspension, which uses canted dampers,
increases rear-wheel travel.

Penton 125

Penton's 125cc Enduro shows the international character of the motorcycle industry. The 125cc Sachs engine originates in West Germany; packed off to Austria, it is finished to KTM specifications and bolted into the Austrian motorcycle. KTM machines are marketed in the United States under the Penton nameplate. This American firm, with deep roots in national and international enduro competition, guides the Austrian company in shaping its products to the tastes of serious off-road riders in America. Those preferences sometimes make the Penton even more international—the Austrian bike uses Italian Ceriani forks.

The pricetag reflects the expertise with which every Penton motorcycle is built. Extraordinarily expensive, the Penton has no appeal to low-budget riders. The 125 Penton's competition credentials make it even less attractive to off-road buffs who ride only on sunny afternoons.

The six-speed Sachs engine has all the instincts of a motocross engine. That's understandable, because the unit is a motocross engine with more effective muffling. The rider must keep the engine at an angry buzz all the time; the unit's real willingness begins at 4,000 rpm, so the rider can't fall back to an easy poke through the woods.

The 125cc Penton—with its snappy engine, chrome-moly cradle frame, Ceriani forks, quick-detachable rear wheel, magnesium hubs, fiberglass tank, and plastic fenders—is an expert's mount in every sense. The lighting kit, which gives a quick nod toward street legality, is just an afterthought.

You'll never find a Penton on the street anyway; look off-road only. Find an enduro in progress, then you'll uncover Pentons by the score.

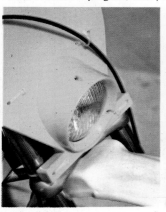 

Rarely are Penton 125 enduro bikes seen with much lighting equipment; far more important are things such as an accurate enduro-type speedometer.

Kawasaki KS-125

Experience improves the breed, and the KS-125 Kawasaki underscores that axiom. For years Kawasaki has been building off-road trail bikes; the old 175cc F7 has been generally recognized as Kawasaki's best example of the trail-bike genre. The KS-125 belongs to a new generation of Kawasaki off-road motorcycles which have been planned and developed in the United States in close cooperation with the parent Japanese company.

Rotary-valve engines once implied bulky powerplants, and bulk is an undesirable feature in an off-road motorcycle. In the KS-125, the Japanese engineers managed to narrow the rotary-valve design without resort to tunnel ports. At the same time, the KS-125 makes horsepower both at high and low rpm. The wide powerband accommodates beginners who need tractable power in the rough, and serves veterans who use high-rpm horsepower to make time off-road. The six-speed gearbox guarantees that all kinds of riders will be able to find an appropriate gear for any situation.

American developers and Japanese engineers tried to keep the KS-125 as trim as practical—though the machine had to meet requirements for street legality in all states. Especially for beginners, the lighter the off-road bike is, the better; every additional pound cruelly taxes the novice rider. Riding an overweight motorcycle off-road is something akin to playing basketball with a medicine ball. At 235 pounds, the KS-125 isn't the lightest 125cc off-roader around, but the figure does keep the bike out of the millstone category.

The stout frame has surprisingly good suspension fore and aft. Since Japanese dual-purpose motorcycles usually skimp on suspension units, the KS-125's excellence may well reflect Kawasaki's stateside program of development. Chalk that up to experience!

The KS-125, like other small enduros, must be tough. Novice trail riders usually bounce off the scenery, but do little maintenance.

Bultaco Alpina

Around some motorcycles tribes of real partisans cluster. The Spanish Bultaco draws such a faithful band: Bultaco enthusiasts know the factory history, model chronology, and peculiarities of certain engines. The faithful treasure the idiosyncrasies of the breed; they willingly understand and explain why individual Bultacos are built in a given way. Perhaps no other European factory could have offered an off-road motorcycle like the 250cc/350cc Bultaco Alpina. Companies without loyal followers may well shun bold novelties.

The Alpina series began as a unique hybrid. Originally a crossbred between a European enduro motorcycle and a genuine trials machine, the Alpina combined low weight, cat-quick steering, and slogger-power. Its two-stroke, single-cylinder engine had power from idling speeds straight to the 5,500-rpm redline. Exceedingly light, the engine could power the bike up a mountain-goat trail, and the fast steering heightened the bike's low-speed agility. Bultaco even engineered a stand-up riding position, à la trials, into the Alpina.

The Alpina's trials-bike characteristics work best in the woods of New England and the Middle West. There the bike's lightning responses allow a rider to pick his way through dense vegetation and pasty mud. Novices might find an Alpina a bit too nervous and over-reactive, though Bultaco experts can play the motorcycle like a fine instrument.

Later Alpina models have had some of their trials features screened out, thus moving the bike closer to the mainstream of European enduro design. Current models have sit-down saddles and slower steering. Nevertheless, the Alpina retains its singular hybrid character—much to the delight of Bultaco enthusiasts. Or anyone who wants to chug along in sure-footed splendor.

Spanish off-road machines have always had a graceful starkness. The Alpina has no gratuitous fripperies.

Kawasaki 175 F7

The Japanese manufacturers are master engine builders. In the power-plant department, the Japanese have repeatedly demonstrated their expertise.

Consider the Kawasaki 175 F7. This rotary-valve, two-stroke single generates an amazing spread of power. The 175cc engine is strong enough in its first 5,000 rpm so that easy-going riders can poke the bike along gently climbing trails. And if the innocent trail leads to a tough, spiky hill with an absolutely grim ascent, the F7-rider can charge the upgrade by spinning the 175cc engine to 8,000 rpm, tap-dancing through the five-speed gearbox, and slipping the clutch if necessary. The Kawasaki power-train can withstand the brutality of such a rough uphill thrash without self-destructing.

The strength of the engine extends beyond horsepower figures and the size of internal ball bearings. In many ways Kawasaki has tried to make the F7 engine as idiotproof as possible. Riders need not remember to close the gasoline tap. The petcock has a vacuum-controlled shut-off; when the engine stops, the tap closes. On the other end of the fuel-delivery system, another pressure-sensitive valve prevents raw gas from entering the crankcase should the bike flop down on its side. Pointless electronic ignition eliminates the vagaries of contract-breaker timing. The oil injection system lubricates the two-stroke engine automatically. The rider must only remember to fill up the oil tank from time to time.

The Kawasaki F7 engine has the character of a first-rate whipping boy—a great capacity for abuse, with little attention required.

The casual trail rider can plonk along easy pathways, paying scant attention to the affable F7, which makes no demands on the rider.

Honda XL-250

Long ago, four-stroke motorcycles became obsolete as first-string off-road bikes. Four-stroke thumpers—as they popped out of their shipping crates—emerged far too heavy and packed too little horsepower, especially when compared to good two-stroke enduro motorcycles. No matter. Honda wrote a success story with its XL-250, a 15-cubic-inch, four-valve single. How could that happen? Simple: most dual-purpose motorcycles roll up much of their mileage on hard-surfaced roads. And on- or off-road, the XL-250 engine is virtually unburstable.

Since 18 horsepower must propel the 300-pound XL-250, the Honda's straight-line performance, on or off the tarmac, can hardly be called dazzling. Those riders who want an agile, lightweight, rapid-fire off-roadster would immediately bypass the XL-250. The Honda thumper has a different orientation. It trades away much of its off-road capability for civility, reliability, and general street-worthiness.

For the pleasure rider who limits his activities to occasional jaunts into cow pastures and along well-defined trails, the XL-250 makes a good sunny-day companion. The willing little Honda has a broad band of power and a great capacity for high-rpm abuse.

Honda's XL-250 is essentially a short-excursion motorcycle which meets the needs of a vast number of enthusiasts. They like dual-purpose motorcycles, but these riders usually stay out of woods and deserts. So the XL-250's street orientation aligns nicely with owner preferences. When he does leave the asphalt byways and follows a meandering cow trail, the XL-250 rider wants a reliable, torquey, mild-mannered vehicle under him. And he gets just that.

77

Beginners love the Honda XL-250;
it may not be a first-line enduro bike, but novice
riders can't abuse it enough to break it.

Can-Am 250 Enduro

Motorcycles may qualify as experts' mounts for many different reasons. Some motorcycles require careful debugging by the owner in the first months of riding. Other bikes may handle so well that fun-day riders are simply unconscious of the machinery's excellence. Still other expert-only motorcycles quickly serve notice to less accomplished riders. The Can-Am 250 Enduro is such a machine.

Most off-road riders prefer engines which can slog along at low engine speeds like a tractor. Nervous, raspy engines (which have little low-speed torque but squirt with high-rpm horsepower) don't endear themselves to many off-road riders—save those expert practitioners who can use a bike with the Can-Am's power characteristics. The rotary-valve two-stroke really comes alive at 5,500 rpm and wields nearly 28 horsepower at 8,000 rpm. This steep power curve demands that the pilot be able to ride rough terrain quickly. So the 250cc Can-Am permits the fast men to go faster—and encourages others to try something else.

Built by the Austrian Rotax company, the Can-Am engine is an extraordinarily narrow rotary-valve design. Rotary induction normally leaves the carburetor huddled under a blister on one side of the engine case. Although rotary-valve induction is a very attractive way to extract a lot of horsepower from a two-stroke engine, the carburetor positioning makes the instrument very vulnerable in rough-and-tumble riding. The Can-Am unit sidesteps this problem with an ingenious ram-tunnel which allows the carburetor to be tucked in safely behind the engine.

The 250 Can-Am Enduro has other earmarks of an expert's motorcycle. Patient development work has produced truly superior front fork and rear suspension units. For those who want to fine-tune handling characteristics, Can-Am bikes have a system for changing the rake and trail of the front fork. It's just another clever feature engineered into this bright-idea motorcycle. And only the experts know how bright!

The Can-Am's gas tank and fenders are molded
in polyethelene, which distorts under impact, then
springs back to normal.

Rokon RT-340

Unique machines in motorcycling have often been bizarre contraptions. Great ideas expressed precisely in blueprints may fall apart when tested in the field. The American-made Rokon RT-340, however, sparkles with unique features that work.

The Rokon looks unconventional. Familiar spoked wheels have no place on the Rokon; cast magnesium alloy wheels carry the tires. Hydraulic disc brakes replace the normal drum-and-shoe stoppers. Powered by a 355cc snowmobile engine, the motorcycle starts with a rewinding pull-cord!

The most distinctive feature of the RT-340 is its "automatic transmission." The Rokon does not employ a conventional clutch and multi-speed transmission. The engine transmits power to a fixed-ratio gearbox **80** by means of a variable-ratio primary drive. Two pulleys, which have

Cast wheels and snowmobile engine
give the Rokon a unique appearance. Pulling
the rewind cable starts the engine.

sides that move in and out, are joined by a V-belt. A system of centrifugal weights and springs in the engine pulley, and a spring-and-cam arrangement at the driven-pulley, permit the speed ratio to change according to engine rpm and rear-wheel traction.

Relieved of shifting, the rider can concentrate totally on the terrain. The Rokon is wonderfully controllable; the frame and suspension deserve much credit for the bike's stability and accuracy.

The variable-ratio drive gives the rider tremendous control of power. An erring pilot may charge up a hill, lose traction, and completely stop in mid-passage. With the Rokon he can turn the power back on again, and the bike will begin to march up the hill—no shifting, no clutch-burning, no engine-killing lurches.

The RT-340 Rokon may well be the harbinger of a new generation of "automatic" off-road machines. Unique motorcycles—with bright ideas that work—richly deserve imitation.

Yamaha DT-400B

Yamaha has devised an appealing compromise with their DT-400B. This 290-pound motorcycle carries all the equipment necessary for street riding, yet the bike has impressive credentials as an off-road mount. The big Yamaha can be tailored to almost any rider preference. Since the DT-400 costs 25 percent less than top-line enduro motorcycles, the demanding off-road enthusiast can afford to upgrade the machine to enduro-competition standards. But owners who occasionally pleasure-ride in rough terrain will find the DT-400B a satisfactory compromise as delivered.

More than anything else, the 397cc engine makes this Yamaha an outstanding machine. Barely churning above idling speed, the power comes flowing out of the reed-valve two-stroke. The Yamaha boasts a formidable torque curve. The low-speed chugging ability enables novice riders almost to forget about shifting, because the Yamaha will slog through sand, chug over ruts and rocks, and tractor up hills without much coaxing. The DT-400 will plow ahead if the engine is running anywhere between 2,000 and 6,000 rpm. The engine's power delivery and its smoothness make the DT-400 Japan's finest enduro engine.

The DT bike won't overwhelm beginners. Yamaha has built the DT-400 on the same general physical scale as 250 enduro motorcycles. Though the rider does pay a weight tax for the extra displacement, the 400cc engine delivers the kind of pulling power which 250cc engines can't produce. Even beginners who can stall broad-powered 250 enduro bikes will find it difficult to bog down and choke off the DT-400B.

Novice off-road riders love the way the DT-400 engine forgives errors. Experienced hands prize the engine as a solid starting point for an off-road special.

Enduro bikes, like the DT-400B, have great ground clearance; a strong bashplate protects the engine.

Maico 400 Qualifier

Only a hard-core devotee of off-road riding would own a Maico 400 Qualifier. It is a pure enduro motorcycle. Although the bike sports lights, muffler, and speedometer, the Maico barely tolerates such trappings. No fancy paint graces the Maico; the 387cc, single-cylinder two-stroke even lacks oil injection. Quality-control and detail-refinement, as practiced in Japan, seem unknown at the German Maico factory.

Maico owners receive something of a kit. The factory bolts all the pieces together in the form of a motorcycle. The enthusiastic owner must actually finish off the product—waterproofing with silicone-seal, and securing all nuts and bolts. The casual motorcyclist could never understand the Maico (or its stratospheric pricetag). But off-road experts really appreciate the German marvel. Why? Because the Maico 400 Qualifier is the best-handling and strongest-running enduro bike that money can buy.

The big piston-port two-stroke churns out steam-engine power. The Maico produces more torque over a greater range of engine speeds than anything in its class—without booster ports or reed-valves. The Qualifier is devoid of common frills in two-stroke engineering.

In all fundamental things, the basic Maico excels. Oil injection may be absent, but Maico constructs its frames with chrome-moly tubing. The 260-pound bike has the best front forks in off-road motorcycling, and the finest-handling chassis. Against such credentials, shoddy paintwork counts for little.

No Maico enthusiast would fritter his Qualifier away on the street. The machine belongs out in the rough where Maico's fabulous engine and running gear make the bike a sensation. Of such stuff are legends made.

A good enduro must be able to motorboat through shallow water without drowning out.

Motocrossers

Two-stroke power dominates the racing world of motocross; in no other corner of motorcycling has this domination been so complete for so long. Two-stroke hegemony has made motocross bikes appear as if they follow a standardized design formula: strong, light-weight frames, which ride on sophisticated suspension components, house single-cylinder, two-stroke engines, which vary in displacement according to class (125cc–500cc). The watchwords for motocross are power, strength, lightness, reliability, handling. The two-stroke racer can best balance these characteristics.

But there are differences, as well as common denominators, in motocross racers. Again and again, manufacturers scrutinize the same basic design elements, searching for better performance. Eye-catching innovations do occur, such as tunnel-port disc-valve engines, or forward-mount shocks, or mono-shock rear suspensions. Other differences and refinements are less apparent. Buried deep inside the equipment, these differences only reveal themselves fully on the track, and then only to the rider.

One engine may have its power concentrated in the mid-range of its rpm band, with no low-rpm power at all. By comparison, another maker's engine might be tuned for far greater low-rpm power, less mid-range urge, and more power near the redline. All other things equal, the layout of the motocross course (relatively flat or hilly) and the track surface (mud, sand, hard dirt) could well determine which engine would work best on a given day. So there's nothing simple about "simple" motocross racers.

The growth of small-displacement motocross racing testifies to the American enthusiasm for the sport and to the success of two-stroke technology. Contemporary 125cc motocrossers make enough power to be genuine racers. Several years ago, no one would have taken 125 racers seriously; today, everyone does. For good reason: four 125cc racers are among the ten best motocrossers in the marketplace.

Neatly lined up in formation, Bultaco team bikes rest in the paddock area before the start of a major motocross event.

125 Can-Am MX-2

In 1970 no one had ever heard of Can-Am motorcycles. The reason was simple: they didn't exist. By 1974 anyone interested in off-road motorcycles knew the Can-Am name. In that brief period Bombardier Limited, builder of Ski-Doo snowmobiles, assembled a design team, developed 125cc and 175cc enduro and motocross machines, ran up an amazing number of competition victories, and began producing motorcycles.

Can-Am competition motorcycles are not single-dimension bikes. They do many things well, but most of all, they make a lot of horsepower. The 125cc Can-Am has been, since its introduction, the horsepower leader of the 125cc motocross class. When other 125cc bikes delivered 16–17 horsepower, the Can-Am developed 20. As its Japanese competitors broke the 20-horsepower barrier, the newest

*Can-Am's reputation was built on the
125/175 MX-1 model, pictured below. The later
MX-2 version has forward-mount shocks.*

version of the Canadian rocketship had a devastating 23 horsepower.

Yet the Can-Am 125 does not win solely on horsepower. The 125 shares much of its running gear with the larger 175 Can-Am's—which means every component is a first-line piece. Can-Am has resisted the logic of economics: cutting production costs by using lower quality materials in smaller engine sizes.

Like other Can-Am products, the 125 MX-2 benefits directly from the factory's involvement in racing. The MX-2 has forward-mount shock absorbers which connect the swinging arm to the frame at points forward of the traditional mounts. The new system, pioneered on works machines, provides greater wheel travel for better control in the rough.

Can-Am works quickly to upgrade its production bikes by applying race department know-how to production-line models. Speed—that's how Can-Am builds instant legends.

Honda CR-125M

Honda's CR-125M comes as a complete motocross package. The owner/rider need not pick the bike apart upon delivery, stacking usable components in one pile and tossing low-quality parts into another heap. By the time they reach the track, many motocrossers are specials composed equally of the original equipment and accessory-house items. But not the Honda.

The Japanese have built the CR-125M with quality components: chromium-molybdenum frame, self-cleaning alloy rims, malleable clutch and brake levers, magnetically-triggered CDI ignition, Keihin racing carburetor, and a number of lightweight alloy castings.

Not only does this single-purpose racing motorcycle look the part, the bike immediately serves the rider notice of its serious intent. The 56mm x 50mm piston-port, reed-valve engine delivers about 19 horsepower and connects to a six-speed transmission. The engine must be kept spinning hard because the horsepower resides inside a narrow band which begins at 7,000 rpm and ends at 9,000 rpm. Given the sharp bulge in its power curve, the Honda motocrosser needs every one of its six speeds.

The rider must be prepared to upshift in rapid-fire sequence when the engine is on the boil. A rider who masters the peaky CR-125M will unconsciously up- and down-shift in harmony with the engine speed. His eyes and mind will be fastened on the track undulations ahead.

A fast, tidy line is important on pint-sized motocrossers. The wrong line can entrap the motorcycle and bog the engine. Once the little two-stroker stumbles out of its powerband, the rider must quickly pick a lower gear to bump the rpm-level back up and retrieve the horsepower.

One-two-five motocrossers like the Honda are demanding machines. When the rider errs, he'll know it.

Honda's first two-stroke came in the
Elsinore series; carefully prepared CR-125M
models can develop 20 horsepower.

Suzuki TM-125 Challenger

World championship motocross was a game that Suzuki learned to play in Europe. The Japanese company grasped the fundamentals quickly and brought world motocross titles back to Japan. Like all large concerns which field competition machines, Suzuki's racing has a commercial impulse. The TM-125 Suzuki Challenger and three other TM-series machines form the business side of motocross racing.

No longer disposable and low-powered play-racers, the 125cc motocrossers have become pretty exotic hardware. The fantastic growth of motocross racing in the United States has made it profitable for the Japanese to build specialized small-displacement racing bikes. And when one Japanese company discovers a new niche in the market, the other majors all rush in.

There are many similarities between the diminutive Japanese motocrossers. For example, the Suzuki and Honda piston-port two-strokes share the same bore and stroke dimensions and fire the spark plugs with electronic-trigger ignitions.

Yet common approaches should not mask very important differences. The Suzuki TM-125 has a much broader spread of power than the Honda 125 motocrosser. Since the Suzuki doesn't have an on-or-off kind of power, its five-speed transmission suffices, allowing the engine to cope with tough terrain. The less demanding engine makes the Suzuki a bit easier for a beginner to handle than a CR-125M Honda.

The power characteristics of the Suzuki engine translate into a lot of traction in the dirt. The Challenger aviates straight and lands true with a competent pilot at the controls. The excellent front fork is backed up by five-position rear shock absorbers.

Thanks to its generous power spread, the TM-125 is a bit easier for beginners to manipulate than very pipey 125's.

Yamaha YZ-125C

Yamaha's YZ-125C sets new marks in the 125 motocross class. Most 125 motocrossers produce 16 to 17 horsepower, measured at the rear wheel on a dynomometer. At 20 horsepower, the Yamaha can over-whelm its Japanese adversaries—assuming, of course, that the YZ-125 is chiming on its pipe (8,500 rpm to 10,500 rpm) and running in the correct gear.

Fundamentally nothing distinguishes the YZ-125C as a powerplant: it's a basic piston-port, two-stroke single—with enough porting to make the cylinder walls look like Swiss cheese. One trick has been a Yamaha characteristic—the reed valve. The company has made successful use of reed valves to strengthen low-end power in many of their models; in the case of the YZ-125C, a huge six-petal reed valve lives between the cylinder and the enormous 30mm carburetor.

The powerband necessitates a six-speed gearbox; to exploit the engine's outstanding horsepower, the rider must row the gear-change lever at a frenzied clip.

The YZ-125C's most obvious innovation is the "mono-shock" rear suspension. The up-and-down movement of the triangulated swing arm is controlled by a single spring and damper unit located under the gasoline tank. Marvelously complex and effective, the unit employs both nitrogen gas and oil to damp movement in both directions. With knowledge and special tools, it's possible for individual riders to adjust the rear suspension to precise individual tastes. By providing a way to increase substantially rear-wheel travel (six-plus inches), the mono-shock system can, properly set up, give superior control in the rough.

Sophisticated as the chassis may be, most Yamaha riders get their edge elsewhere—with that 20-horsepower engine!

95

The mono-shock Yamaha appears a bit odd, since the cantilever shock-absorbers are obviously missing.

Honda CR-250M

For more than a decade, Honda tied itself to four-stroke technology. All Hondas covered ground with four-stroke power. But major manufacturers relentlessly pursue sales success, and in that pursuit, Honda's exclusive four-stroke loyalty ended. When Honda moved into two-stroke power in 1973, their thrust came in motocross, the strongest preserve of two-stroke machinery.

The introduction of the CR-250M Elsinore demonstrated Honda's determination to carve out an important chunk of the motocross business. The Elsinore 250 hardly amazed the motorcycle world with any great technical innovations. The new bike rested on concepts already battle-tested in other motocrossers. The powerplant was quite orthodox: a high-quality, piston-port engine wedded to a close-ratio transmission. The 29-horsepower engine immediately placed the bike in the front ranks of motocross machinery.

The pricetag of the Elsinore has never fully reflected the quality of its construction. Frame material is 4130 chrome-moly tubing, and the tube-work creates the basis for a very light, strong motorcycle. The engine contains some expensive magnesium castings, while the gas tank has been rendered in aluminum. Weight-conscious construction has produced a 225-pound motocrosser, a figure which draws the envy of competitors.

Motorcycling has many bargains, and the 250 Elsinore certainly qualifies as one. In any sport, buying more for less is always fun.

Elsinore was the first two-stroke Honda seen by American enthusiasts. Many had thought Honda was "four-stroke forever"—wrong!

Montesa 250 Cappra VR

Motorcycling is full of "replica racers," some real and others fictitious. When a factory develops a competitive motorcycle in national or international racing, the company often decides to capitalize on the model's success by marketing a replica. Many motorcycles, ostensibly genuine copies of factory competition bikes, roll off the production line as faint shadows of the real thing, or simply victims of strict cost accounting. Occasionally, the genuine article is faithfully replicated, and the result is a motorcycle like the 250 Montesa Cappra VR.

As a factory racer, the Montesa did not win a world championship. In 1972 the Spanish concern did make an excellent showing in world class competition with Finnish rider Kalevi Vehkonen. Shortly thereafter, the 250cc Montesa Cappra Vehkonen Replica appeared.

The Montesa hasn't an ounce of nonsense on it. Though it weighs in at 230 pounds wet, the most impressive numbers are those figures which come out of the engine. The two-stroke single can sting its competition with an honest 30 horsepower at the rear wheel. That puts the Montesa in the forefront of 250 production motocrossers. The torque curve complements the horsepower chart: a gentle curve runs from 6,000 rpm to 8,000 rpm.

Tough seasons on the grand prix circuit have produced a running gear with outstanding handling. Montesa has tuned the front fork and the cantilever rear suspension perfectly to the stout frame. The motorcycle tracks beautifully and refuses to yaw when squirted wide open.

Skimming over rough terrain in full flight, the Cappra VR proves its replica label is no hollow boast.

Cappra VR benefits from Montesa's race testing; the works bike shown here has the latest cantilever rear suspension.

250 Can-Am MX-2

Can-Am has aimed their 250cc MX-2 at the serious expert. Everything about this motorcycle—the phenomenal power it produces, the quality of its components, the engineering knowledge inside it, the size of its pricetag—testifies to the earnest intentions of the manufacturer.

Consider the power output of Can-Am's tunnel-port, rotary-valve, two-stroke engine. Most 250cc motocrossers pick up 50 percent in horsepower over a 2,000–2,500 rpm band. Typically, a strong moto-crosser might develop about 20 horsepower at 5,000 rpm and 30 horse-power at 7,500 rpm, and that 50-percent escalation requires a skillful rider.

Then there's the 250 Can-Am. Twenty horsepower arrives at the rear wheel at 6,000 rpm; when the engine peaks at 8,600 rpm, a shattering 34 horsepower reaches the ground. Across 2,600 rpm the power in-creases 70 percent! With 10 percent more maximum power than other 250 production motocross bikes, the Can-Am catapults forward with an explosive surge. A good dirt jockey will come closer to flying the 250 Can-Am than riding it.

The horsepower propels very little dead weight. Though the Can-Am has built the frame and swinging arm with mild steel rather than chrome-moly, the race-ready weight totals 230 pounds—hardly porky by motocross standards. Magnesium alloy engine cases, clutch and ignition covers, wheel hubs and backing plates help pare down the weight.

The frame and running gear is as highly developed as the engine. Riders can alter the fork angle by using the adjustment system in the steering head. The forward-mount shock absorber system represents the current state of the art; the rear suspension incorporates Can-Am racing lessons from the 1974 season.

100   Power, handling, and race-breeding—the MX-2 has it all.

The MX-2 has been built on the race-proven premise that the best riders go faster with high-rpm horsepower rather than low-rpm torque.

101

CZ 400

Almost a decade ago, CZ revolutionized 500cc world championship motocross. In 1966, after two years of development, the Czechoslovakian company snatched the 500 World Championship with a 360cc two-stroke single. Thus began the upheaval in the senior class—and one which drove the four-stroke singles into oblivion.

Production-line motocrossers from CZ have their origins in the firm's grand prix bikes. In the late nineteen-sixties Belgian Joel Robert won two 250cc titles on motorcycles much like CZ's over-the-counter motocrosser, introduced in 1968.

When the CZ company launches a new motocross bike, the machine begins its production run at the cutting edge of technology. In order to keep the machinery competitive with later designs, CZ refines its equipment under a long-range development program. That's unlike the Japanese approach, which hurries a completely new design right in behind an existing model.

Three current CZ motocrossers—125, 250, and 400—share the same basic running gear; the engines, though similar, are quite distinct units. At 250 pounds wet, the smaller-displacement bikes have gradually become "heavy" motocrossers as their newer competitors have shed weight. But CZ's 381cc two-stroke single carries its 250 pounds without difficulty. Sometimes, if manufacturers can't slim down a motorcycle, they can slip in a larger engine. The stronger an engine, the more gracefully it bears weight. And so for many riders the 400 CZ works better than its 250 counterpart.

The gradual increase in horsepower and displacement over the years has dictated suspension and chassis modifications. Detail changes, for example, have slowed down the traditional steering-quickness of CZ motocrossers.

Thanks to constant refinement, the manufacturer that started the two-stroke revolution in big-bore motocross still reaps the commercial benefits.

As direct descendants of world championship winning machinery, CZ motocrossers are tough, brutal bikes programmed to win.

Maico 400 MX

Raw specifications, spelled out on blueprint paper, can deceive. Maicos are confounding motorcycles; they befuddle those who think engineering trickery automatically produces first-place trophies. On paper, the Maico 400cc motocrosser is almost unassuming; yet, on the track, the bike can be unbeatable. Many enthusiasts believe it is the finest big-bore motocrosser available to private competition riders.

No production motocrosser outhandles the 400cc Maico; nevertheless, Maico uses one basic chrome-moly frame for all the company's motocross and enduro bikes in every displacement category. Logic says a universal frame shouldn't work, but in the Maico case it does. Maico **104** forks, recognized as *the* standard, hold no intricate secrets in valving,

damping, or springing. Fork superiority rests on materials and assembly.

The brutishly powerful 400cc motocrosser has an absolutely diminutive four-speed gearbox, originally designed for the first 125cc Maico long ago. Yet this transmission still serves well in the super-power Maico motocrossers. In a day when two-stroke technology includes booster ports, reed valves, electronic ignition, disc valves, and hundreds of little touches, the Maico remains embarrassingly simple—and produces awesome power over a wide powerband.

Maico motorcycles are the products of a small German factory which specializes in competition mounts. Like any other Maico machine, the 400cc motocrosser is poorly finished by Japanese standards. Rough-hewn the Maico may be, but there's nothing at all crude about winning.

105

Maico hasn't been styled into a
rugged, angular appearance; it's just
the result of functional engineering.

•6
American Championship Motorcycles

The chase for the American Grand National Motorcycle Championship begins in February in Houston, Texas. The chase has 20-odd races, spread out over nine months and all parts of the country. When the grind ends in October, racers have driven thousands of miles, thousands of spectators have seen hundreds of racing miles, and everyone knows who the new National Champion is.

The National Champion has spent the year demonstrating his cold-nerved skill in four categories: steeplechase, dirt short track, mile and half-mile dirt track, and road racing. Any champion must be master of both road racing and mile/half-mile competition because these events account for 75 percent of the national championship meets.

No hopeful can go racing on the national circuit without a bank vault full of equipment. Each type of racing has its own intricate, specialized machinery. Road racing bikes would be entirely alien on a dirt track, and a flat tracker an equal foreigner on any pavement circuit. The racer himself provides the link between all categories: he must be at ease pitching his dirt tracker sideways at 100 mph on a mile oval, and just as cool-headed as rushing toward a 120-mph bend at 170 mph on his road racer.

Money fuels racing in America. For manufacturers and distributors victory is a matter of prestige and honor. A few manufacturers are willing to pay handsomely for a winning image and this means bearing the cost of factory teams and professional riders.

But the heaviest investment is the creation, development, and refinement of complex, exotic racing hardware. This war of engineering never ends. The struggle behind the scenes begins before the season opens, and continues without interruption. Twenty-odd races merely punctuate the war fought at the drawing boards.

Yankee motorcycle racing grew up on horse tracks; this racing is still the most intense and hardest fought in America.

Harley-Davidson XR-750

Though seriously challenged every season, Harley-Davidson's XR-750 V-twin remains the dominant force in American dirt-track racing. At mile and half-mile ovals, the Harley twins are implicit favorites. Indeed, the deference shown to the Milwaukee twins at dirt tracks is much like the respect given to Yamaha TZ-700's at road races. Other machines don't simply win dirt-track events; they must beat the Harley V-twins.

Individual dirt-track machines, though nominally alike, reflect the studied preferences of given pilots. At speed, expert riders can detect small variations in basic frame geometry, suspension action, tire patterns, and a score of other areas. Riders become sensitive to incremental changes which may produce a winning edge—because dirt-oval contests are fierce, intense, close-quartered battles. The difference between winning and finishing tenth could hinge on tire selection.

Unlike its competitors, the Harley-Davidson XR-750 is no hybrid racer, in which a modified production engine mates to a special dirt-track frame. In its primary mode, the XR-750 was designed as a dirt-track racing bike. As a pure racer built with a specific purpose, the V-twin enjoys the advantages inherent in machines developed from clean drawing paper.

The XR-750's metal technology runs far beyond standard light alloy castings. The cylinders and cylinderheads are cast in a space-age aluminum alloy with an unusually high silver content; this light, tough material quickly dissipates the heat generated at racing speeds.

Painstaking development went into the cylinderhead design; the effort exceeded any reasonable level for general purpose motorcycle engines. The configuration of intake and exhaust ports could follow the dictates of flow-bench testing; compromises for mass production weren't necessary. And so, with development, the best XR-750 engines have produced 80 horsepower.

Yet dirt-track races cannot be won with sheer power. A victory takes many elements—stability, traction, reliability, and power. And that mixture consistently sends the pushrod Harley twin to the winner's circle.

109

Factory-backed XR-750 boasts such refinements as magnesium artillery wheels—and brilliant rider Gary Scott.

Yamaha 750

More than its adversaries, the Yamaha 750cc dirt-tracker is an assemblage. The Yamaha is not a racing bike designed from scratch, such as the Harley-Davidson XR-750. And the Yamaha 750 engine, unlike the Triumph and Norton units, has no roadster counterpart. Yamaha's 750cc vertical twin has been created from the 650cc roadster engine.

Construction of such an engine means careful selection of parts. Early-series Yamaha 650 crankcases—lighter and less complex than later series—form the foundation of the 750cc special. All non-essentials are deleted. For example, in the absence of a generator, a total-loss battery system supplies ignition current. The 650cc engine grows to 750cc with modified cylinders, oversized liners, and 80mm pistons which replace the standard 75mm items. Cylinderhead modifications include racing camshaft, re-profiled ports, and larger valves. Big

carburetors and tuned-megaphone exhausts round out the package. This speed-kit was developed in the United States because dirt-track racing, as practiced by Yankees, is indigenous to America.

This bolt-up hot rod serves well on mile and half-mile tracks. The Yamaha trackers have an impressive spread of power. The single-overhead-camshaft engine has about 65 horsepower at 7,000 rpm and returns a solid 70 horsepower at 8,500 rpm, the logical rev-limit for the nine-piece, pressed-together crankshaft.

Champion, a frame specialist, supplies the structures used by factory-supported Yamaha 750's. But with more and more privateers switching to Yamaha power, every frame-master has a chassis for Yamaha's ever-present twin. The specialists just might be playing their hunches: with increasing stateside development of the Japanese vertical twin, the Yamaha 650-to-750 unit may yet become the dominant force on American dirt tracks.

111

AMA Champion Kenny Roberts shows
his winning blend of courage, equilibrium,
power, traction, and concentration.

Norton 750

Triumph's vertical twin has been a stalwart of mile and half-mile racing for a quarter-century. First as a 500cc racer, and later in 650cc and 750cc versions, the Triumph twin has powered a long line of successful dirt-trackers. But when the factory discontinued production of 750cc twins, the end of the works-supported dirt-trackers became inevitable. Unquestionably, privateers will continue with Triumph power for several seasons, so the Triumph name will not disappear on the dirt tracks.

Neither will another British vertical twin. The Triumph's stablemate, Norton, will continue to battle Yamaha and Harley-Davidson with full factory support. Norton has a promising future as a dirt-track racer; the current long-stroke engine already produces competitive horsepower, and the short-stroke Norton 750cc engine will guarantee that British vertical twins remain competitive.

Norton's 73mm x 89mm powerplant develops around 68–70 horsepower at 7,000 rpm, and like the Triumph twin, the Norton pulls strongly from 4,500–5,000 rpm. With a more robust crankshaft assembly, the Norton twin can endure more strain without breaking than the old Triumph engine.

Frame specialists build the running chassis for most mile and half-mile racers. Trackmaster, one of the California specialists, constructs frames to the specifications of the Norton factory team. The most unusual feature of the single-loop Norton/Trackmaster frame is its notch in the central tube; this hump allows the cylinderhead to be removed for servicing without pulling the complete engine from the frame.

The wheelbase measures about 56 inches, though the rear axle can be moved 1 or 2 inches in a horizontal plane and also adjusted in vertical plane in order to vary the handling for particular race tracks. The fork angle can be varied from 27 to 28 degrees.

Handlebar bends and foot-peg positions must be fit to an individual rider, according to his own style, strength, and physical size. And that's fair enough. Any racer needs the confidence which comes from a perfect fit.

113

Works-supported Triumph dirt-trackers (above) have been terminated. British honor will ride solely on the Norton name (below).

Yamaha TZ-250

For a decade, the Yamaha 250 road racers have been the dominant force in American lightweight road racing. Yamaha broke the ranks of its 250cc opponents—Parilla, Ducati, Honda, Benelli, Bultaco, Suzuki, Kawasaki—and one by one they disappeared.

Inside a ten-year period, Yamaha introduced no less than seven series of 250cc racers, each more powerful and reliable than its forerunner. By comparison, other manufacturers seemed far less ambitious. Every one or two years Yamaha widened their technological gap by building new equipment.

The Yamaha TD-1A of 1963 was an air-cooled, piston-port two-stroke with 27mm carburetors, magneto ignition, a wide-ratio five-speed gearbox and sometimes-exploding clutch. Speed, not reliability, was the A-model's strength. Piston seizures would stop many TD-1A's. Yamaha had not yet perfected the wall coating for its aluminum-alloy

114

*A generation of racers, including
American Champion Kenny Roberts, learned their
craft aboard Yamaha 250 twins.*

cylinders, and at speed the pistons often jammed in the cylinders. If it lasted, the A-model—with 29 horsepower at 9,500 rpm and 118 mph in top speed—was the fastest lightweight around.

Yamaha's TZ-250 shows ten years of progress. Piston/cylinder compatibility was solved long ago. The water-cooled, twin-cylinder racer turns out about 54 horsepower and runs 30 miles per hour faster than the TD-1A. Expansion chamber developments and piston/cylinder porting advances account for the phenomenal increase in performance. Thirty-four-millimeter carburetors feed the 11,000-rpm engine, while pointless electronic ignition triggers the spark plugs. Engine power reaches the rear wheel via a dry clutch and six-speed close-ratio transmission. The TZ-250 handles corners in a way that TD-1A owners would never have believed possible. The super-effective front disc brake stops the TZ-250 far better than the A-model managed with its twin-cam drum brake.

The TZ-250 exhibits determined work and winning experience. **115**

Harley-Davidson RR-250

Harley-Davidson returned to the lightweight road-racing arena in 1974. Absent for three years following the demise of its old 250/350 four-stroke single, the Milwaukee firm rejoined the battle with two-stroke twin-cylinder power. Its new RR-250, a production version of the works Harley-Davidson, is a near-replica of the world-championship bike used by Walter Villa.

In its 1974 American début, the RR-250 gave the Yamaha camp an intense, if short, fit. In the hands of Harley-Davidson ace Gary Scott, the surprisingly powerful Italian racer motored away from Kenny Roberts and his nearly invincible water-cooled Yamaha. Scott's win at Loudon, New Hampshire snapped an unbroken procession of Yamaha 250 victories. Subsequent mechanical problems and team injuries prevented the Italian water-pumper from posting any other wins in 1974. Nevertheless, by the season's closer at Ontario, California, the works and semi-works Harley-Davidson 250's had become the fastest lightweights in America.

Under new AMA rules, only 25—instead of 200—RR-250's needed to be built in order to qualify the model for American racing. The old 200-unit rule had effectively quashed any American racing plans by manufacturers who had small facilities for race-bike production. The Italian division of Harley-Davidson had no way of meeting the 200-bike rule. But production of 25 units was possible.

As the Harley-Davidson RR-250's began to filter into private hands, lightweight racing regained some spectator interest. With the 25-unit rule, updated Yamahas and brand new Kawasaki 250's seem certain to appear. Two-fifty racing in America may once again become a real battle of brands.

Though its basic engine specifications resemble the Yamaha TZ-250, the RR-250's general appearance is quite different.

Suzuki 750

The Suzuki 750 water-cooled road racer has its origins in the GT-750 touring machine. Unlike Yamaha, which met AMA rules with 200 examples of the TZ-700, the Suzuki 750 racer began, in theory at least, as a roadster and became—by the magic of piece-by-piece replacement—a racer.

First seen in 1972, the water-cooled triple proved awesomely powerful. Suzuki had the first 750 with a genuine 100 horsepower. That sort of power revealed handling deficiencies which were latent in lesser machines. Plagued by homologation infractions, low reliability levels, and handling difficulties, the Suzuki team labored through the 1972/73 seasons, usually showing far more potential than positive results.

Suzuki built new racing bikes for 1974 and launched a development program in the United States. Early encouragement in 1974 (near-victory at Daytona, an outright win at Loudon) turned to gloom when injuries benched Suzuki's fastest rider, Gary Nixon. His absence

In the United States, repeated
victories have fallen just beyond Suzuki's grasp,
despite star riders like Paul Smart.

also halted the development of the semi-works Erv Kanemoto-750 Suzuki, which was clearly the best-prepared and most potent Suzuki racer in the United States.

The 70mm x 64mm three-cylinder engine produces maximum horsepower at about 8,000 rpm. Thanks to its good breathing characteristics and water cooling, the Suzuki develops more horsepower at 8,000 rpm than the air-cooled Kawasaki does at 9,500 rpm. For sheer horsepower, the Suzuki proved equal to the Yamaha TZ-700, though the lack of a six-speed transmission handicapped the Suzuki many times in 1974.

Under new, liberalized AMA rules, a revamped water-cooled Suzuki will be able to maintain its horsepower parity with the Yamaha TZ-700. Indeed, with 100-plus horsepower on command, all camps will be carefully studying frame design. Both Yamahas and Suzukis have ample power; the trick is building a frame to contain the juggernaut engines.

Kawasaki 750 H2R

Kawasaki's air-cooled H2R 750cc road racer reached the end of its development in 1974. When it first appeared in 1972, the three-cylinder bike immediately became the machine to watch—and shortly thereafter, the thing to beat in the AMA national road-racing series. Modified and updated for the 1973 season, Kawasaki remained the major power at almost any road race in North America. Rolling on cast magnesium "artillery wheels," and painted in high-visibility green, the Kawasakis could easily be picked out in any collection of 750 racing equipment.

Time deals harshly with racing motorcycles. The 1974 AMA season brought updated Suzuki racers and the new Yamaha TZ-700. These water-cooled wonders made the Kawasaki H2R show its age. Based on the air-cooled 750 Kawasaki roadster, the H2R racer could not be converted to water cooling under the AMA rules then in force. Yet a water-cooled racer was necessary to keep Kawasaki competitive.

A completely new water-cooled engine would give Kawasaki an opportunity to update transfer-port design, thus increasing horsepower. But fundamentally, water cooling prevents that horsepower loss which occurs in all air-cooled two-strokes as they reach hot operating temperatures. A 92-horsepower, air-cooled Kawasaki 750, when fully warmed up, could skid back down to 78 horsepower.

The 71mm x 63mm air-cooled triple, spinning to 9,500 rpm and feeding its power through a five-speed gearbox, would fairly catapult the lightweight (310 pounds dry) Kawasaki out of corners. Experiments in 1974 included larger 38mm carburetors (to raise the output) and a revised frame (to obtain better handling). But these were small steps compared to the obvious next stage, water cooling.

A revision of the AMA rulebook will enable Kawasaki to develop a water-cooled successor to the H2R. And that should make the Green Meanies from Kawasaki front-line contenders again.

121

Yvon du Hamel, Kawasaki's team leader,
has ridden the H2R to more major American
victories than any other rider.

Yamaha TZ-700

In one short season Yamaha became the ruling power in AMA big-bike road racing. Though the old 350cc Yamaha twins had occasionally whipped their 750 opposition through 1973, the new TZ-700 Yamaha locked up AMA road racing by the end of 1974. In order to meet the old AMA homologation rule, Yamaha produced 200 racers, and these 700cc four-cylinder water-cooled machines were virtually grand prix machines, which were made available to privateers.

The 700 racer is a juggernaut. Essentially two 350cc water-cooled twins lashed together, the four-cylinder in its original version produced some 90 horsepower in a relatively mild state of tune. Reed-valves and fairly modest exhaust port-timing made the engine tractable. Even so, 90 horsepower—fed through a six-speed transmission—produced heart-stopping acceleration. Ninety horsepower was just the beginning for the 370-pound motorcycle as the exigencies of racing and normal development pushed the output well beyond the century mark.

At first many privateers believed that the big Yamaha would be far easier to ride than the TZ-350 production racer, which most private entrants had earlier used. The smaller bike had that famous on/off light-switch type of power. But riders soon discovered that the four-cylinder two-stroke made other demands, equally exacting as the twins. With such terrific power on call, riders had to develop a very sensitive throttle hand because the TZ-700 could literally spin the rear tire coming out of corners. Riding hard at the limit, the slightest miscue could pitch the complete plot into the weeds. The big Yamaha's fantastic power did not operate as a great leveling tool among riders. Rather, the 100-horsepower monsters served to elevate more quickly that natural aristocracy of racing talent.

Of all the American riders, no one raced the 700 Yamaha with more skill, finesse, and élan than AMA National Champion Kenny Roberts. In Europe, England, and America Roberts underscored that proposition
again and again in 1974.

Two great Yamaha riders: Kenny Roberts (black and yellow American team bike) and Giacomo Agostini (red and white European bike).

Amateur racing is the backbone of motocross in America. Thousands of fun-day riders compete in hundreds of local events which reward success with trophies, not money. But at the very top, motocross racing has gone professional in the United States. The business of racing has become too competitive, too intense, too prestigious to be left to amateurs.

Three national titles draw big-league sponsors, professional riders, and factory teams—the National Motocross Championships in the 125cc, 250cc, and 500cc classes. Only native Yankees can compete in this national series staged by the American Motorcycle Association.

Two other series open events to European professionals. The first is the brief mid-summer Inter-AMA for 250cc motorcycles; 500cc motocrossers run in the longer Trans-AMA series. By the time the Trans-AMA calendar begins in late September, the FIM world championships have been settled, and many international stars hop over to America to campaign in the Yankee races. About ten events make up the Trans-AMA, thus enthusiasts from New York to California can see world-champion riders. The international stars give the spectators (and the domestic opposition) some dazzling lessons in the art of motocross racing.

Money brings the world pros to America. The entire pay-off amounts to more than the winning purses. The manufacturers—who sponsor professional riders—have a great stake in the American series: four out of five motocross bikes are sold in the Yankee marketplace.

Sunday's spectators, the manufacturers reason, are Monday's customers in a land where enthusiasts cheer with their wallets.

*Masterful riders and superb machines
give motocross racing a fluid grace
far above the violent terrain.*

Honda RC-125

Racing is serious business for Honda. The largest motorcycle manufacturer in the world cannot go racing merely for fun. As the richest and grandest motorcycle producer, Honda must win. When small companies achieve victories, that's spectacular news. When Honda wins, it's almost expected. And Honda did win the 125cc American Motocross Championship in 1974, as Marty Smith scooped up the title with a works Honda.

The RC-125 is a factory-racing special, quite distinct from the over-the-counter CR-125. The works Honda scales in at the legal FIM minimum weight—178 pounds. That's not unusual for a factory bike, but Honda held a clear advantage in the horsepower department. Only the Can-Am 125 threatened Honda horsepower in 1974. Honda's magnesium/chrome-moly/titanium masterpiece went to the starting line with well over 20 horsepower—perhaps 25 horsepower—in its crankcase/reed induction engine.

Honda's induction system does not feed into the cylinder, the standard practice when the piston controls the intake timing. Rather, the inlet pathway leads directly into the crankcase, and crankcase pressure and the reed valve govern the timing of the intake charge. Honda claims the unique system produces the low-rpm power of a normal reed-valve engine and the high-rpm power associated with piston-port designs which have no reed valves.

Honda also spent much time working on suspension tuning. And that meant adjusting damper positioning and spring/damper action. Even with a horsepower bonus, Honda could not ignore suspension development, because superior handling in the rough often determines the winning margin. And in 1974, Honda had the right combination of reliability, handling, power—and riding talent. With that blend, Honda did the expected.

The RC-125 is a light and spindly 178 pounds. The FIM imposes minimum weight limits in the interest of safety and fair competition.

Can-Am 250 GP

By the end of 1974 some pundits thought Gary Jones had taken the AMA's 250cc National Motocross Championship out on permanent loan. The young Californian won the title for the third straight year; to date Jones has been the only rider to hold the 250 crown since its creation. Yet every year, he has claimed the title on a different machine, and in 1974 Jones was Can-Am mounted.

The Can-Am 250cc grand prix bike underwent constant changes throughout the season. At virtually every major round in the AMA championship, the bike was different. Seemingly, there was but one permanent equation in the Can-Am formula—the 4130 chrome-moly chassis and its geometry—and this stayed intact. Otherwise, Can-Am modified race to race, experimenting with fork-rake angles, springs, and damping. That was only the beginning.

More fundamental modifications also occurred. The shock absorber placement proceeded from a standard vertical position to a forward-mount location. In its final pattern, the rear suspension allowed 6 inches of rear-wheel travel. Can-Am swapped dampers around, starting with S&W units, moving to Koni hydraulics, and finally settling on Girling gas-oil components.

Without question, the Can-Am GP was the fastest 250 on the AMA motocross tour. Its power reflected much detailed work. Inside the engine cases, cast entirely in magnesium, each gear in the five-speed transmission was drilled and machined for lightness. Though Jones' early-season bike showed 34 horsepower on the dynamometer, new expansion chambers, modified port timing and different rotary valves pushed the output to 39 horsepower at the season's end.

And for Gary Jones, that was all he needed.

In 1974 Can-Am took a moderate approach in suspension, opting for forward-mount shocks rather than a cantilever system.

Kawasaki KX-400

Sometimes less is more. Consider the gradually decreasing displacement of some 500 motocrossers. The Kawasaki which carried Jim Weinert to the 1974 AMA 500cc Motocross Championship reflected this downward movement. The works KX-motocrosser began the season with a 450cc two-stroke engine and finished with a 401cc motor. The smaller two-stroke revved higher and made more horsepower, though it lacked the low-rpm torque and pulling power of the larger displacement engine. But top-flight motocross riders can go faster with more horsepower.

By the season's end, the 401cc engine possessed abundant power. In its latest version, the two-stroke rings in hard at 4,500 rpm; at 7,000 rpm, the engine peaks, producing 45 horsepower at the rear wheel. When the engine reaches its powerband, the bike simply rockets forward. Even an accomplished amateur rider would find the Kawasaki unmanageable. But star-professionals can govern such bikes, and for that kind of touch, factories must—and do—pay.

The running gear, as well as the engine, is calibrated for extraordinary riders. There's a day-and-night difference between the handling of the 217-pound works bike and the production motocrosser. The front suspension gives a full 8 inches of travel while the laydown shock absorbers permit the rear axle to move up and down more than 7.5 inches. The ordinary rider would find the suspension of the factory racer far too stiff. However, if he could go fast enough through rough terrain, he'd find out what the professional already knows: the suspension is just **130** soft enough!

Development never stops on works motocrossers. The Trans-AMA bike was a further development of the AMA 500cc title winner.

Suzuki 400

If anyone knows how to win in world championship motocross, it's Roger De Coster. The Belgian rider joined the Suzuki motocross team in 1971 with spectacular results. He won the 500cc FIM crown three years straight, 1971–72–73. Machine problems repeatedly slowed or stopped his Suzuki in 1974, and his 500 title slipped away.

A veteran of the fall Trans-AMA circuit, De Coster returned to America in 1974. Both he and his Suzuki were in peak form, and the Trans-AMA title easily fell to De Coster. His autumn-series bike was quite similar to the Suzuki grand prix machine as developed late in the European season. The troublesome 370cc GP engine was replaced with **132** a production-based 396cc two-stroke. De Coster and Sylvain Geobeors

designed and constructed a new one-off frame around the 396cc powerplant which came from a TM-400 Cyclone.

The cantilever rear suspension, with a heavily gusseted swing arm,
operates with Japanese Kayaba gas-oil shock absorbers, which give a
tremendous amount of rear-wheel travel. The front fork tubes, Kayaba
units with 7.5 inches of movement, could be set in any one of three
different triple-clamps. The clamp changes provide a gross adjustment;
the handling characteristics of a good GP bike can be fine-tuned in a
half-dozen places.

With the Trans-AMA trophy and prize money in hand, De Coster
could return to the 1975 world championship events with his reconsti-
tuted Suzuki motocrosser and renewed hope. It just could be 1971 all
over again in 1975.

133

*De Coster rides the 396cc Suzuki with an
urbane smoothness. Totally unruffled, he guides
the bike, which rockets in a frenzy.*

Maico 400

Not only does the Trans-AMA series close off one international grand prix season, but it also begins another. In the 1974 American "finale" Maico riders and technicians experimented with different modifications and set-ups, in an attempt to sort out their machinery for the 1975 grand prix season in Europe.

To discover what *won't* work is often just as important as the inverse. For European marques, losing a Trans-AMA motocross race is far less serious than dropping a World Championship event. So the United States series makes an ideal testing ground for companies like Maico: all the world-class competitors—racing hard in America—provide good yardsticks.

Maico, for example, tried new port timing specifications which produced tremendous high-rpm horsepower. Sheer horsepower wasn't the answer; that approach fit neither machine nor rider. Maico discarded the experimental porting in favor of the standard 1974 design.

The Trans-AMA Maicos were trick in other ways. Revised forks, with 8 inches of travel, attached to a new frame, which featured Maico's version of the cantilever rear suspension system. Gas-oil rear shocks allowed 8 inches of movement in the alloy swing arm. Even though good handling has long been a trademark of the conventional Maico running gear, the German manufacturer clearly intends to run up front in the motocross-suspension revolution.

At the end of the 1974 Trans-AMA series, Maico's Adolph Weil finished third. It was a good third, one which gave Maico a running start on the 1975 grand prix season.

Trans-AMA Maicos had drastic alterations
in the rear suspension and more subtle
changes in the engine.

Husqvarna 360 CR Mikkola Replica

While some manufacturers use the Trans-AMA series to prepare for the following year's grand prix season, other companies showcase their new models during the American tour. In 1974 Husqvarna raced new production models named after Heikki Mikkola and his world-title motocrosser.

In many ways the production-line 360cc Husqvarna, ridden in the Trans-AMA events by Heikki Mikkola, Arne Kring, and Brad Lackey, was a better machine than the grand prix motorcycle on which it was based. The production 360 CR Husky incorporates all things that worked in Europe, and nothing that didn't.

The chassis follows the same geometry as the Mikkola grand prix machine without the excessive gusseting of the world-title bike. The Swedish factory heat-treats its frames before welding and then normalizes them after fabrication; this process minimizes frame flexing and

breakage. The suspension is likewise built for roughery. Up front the production bike rides on a Husqvarna fork with 7.5 inches of travel, and in the rear Girling gas-oil shocks provide bump control.

The present 360cc engine grew out of Husqvarna's old 400cc four-speed unit. The smaller displacement engine has a narrower bore and shorter connecting rod. Engine cases are cast in magnesium, and so are the clutch hub and plates. A 36mm Bing carburetor feeds into the aluminum cylinder where the Femsa ignition system fires off the fuel-air charge. The explosion is considerable because the 360cc engine produces an incredible 39 horsepower with standard-specification porting. The big-number horsepower implies a relatively tight powerband, but there's a six-speed gearbox to help cope with the power curve.

Launched in the 1974 Trans-AMA series where it finished behind Japanese and European works bikes, Husky's new 360 proved itself a winner nonetheless. In a fitting victory, Heikki Mikkola guided the 360 to its first major American win.

137

Husky's 360 has a look of purpose;
it's as functional as a cannonball With 39
horsepower, it's not much slower.

•8
World Championship Motorcycles

World championship motorcycles fall into two broad categories, road racing and motocross. The FIM *(Federation Internationale Motocycliste)* awards six world titles in road racing and three world championships in motocross. As a corollary, the FIM calculates manufacturers' championships in world title competition. Almost always constructors' championships follow the individual titles. For example, in 1974 Giacomo Agostini won the 350 World Championship in Road Racing on a Yamaha; after the season's points had been tallied, Yamaha earned the 350 Constructor's title.

The FIM hands out world prizes in areas other than road racing and motocross, but such titles are minor league in comparison. These additional titles are: Team Speedway, Individual Speedway, Best Pair Speedway, 1,000-Meter Sand Track, Ice Racing, and Trials.

Traditionally the FIM rulebook has been very thin. World championship bikes, in motocross and road racing, need not be based on production-line models. Manufacturers who are major contenders normally build ultra-special one-off racers. Consequently, in the world-title series, enthusiasts will see the grandest monuments to no-expense-spared engineering. In efforts to stay competitive, factories may substitute one experimental bike for another from one grand prix to the next.

Those who love to scrutinize lavish racing hardware always find something new to see at every event; but though one may gawk in the paddocks, the observer will not likely gather much hard information. Factory mechanics and riders stay tight-lipped about equipment changes. "This engine," quipped one mechanic, patting the latest factory racer, "is a model of uncertain dimensions built out of unobtanium."

138

With his title on the line, 125 World Champion Kent Andersson rockets out front on his water-cooled Yamaha twin.

MV Agusta 500

In 1974 MV Agusta carried Phil Read to his second consecutive 500 World Championship in Road Racing. The Italian maker, which has practically owned the 500 championship series since 1958, faced its most serious challengers in seven years—Giacomo Agostini and the Yamaha four-cylinder road racer.

The MV Agusta is the most competitive four-stroke solo bike in world series racing. Generally, four-stroke engines make less horsepower than two-stroke designs of comparable size—and four-strokes are far heavier and more expensive to build. Despite the odds, MV Agusta pressed ahead in 1974, and won.

The double-overhead-camshaft engine, with four valves per cylinder, produced over 90 horsepower at a fantastic 16,000 rpm. Bore and stroke measure 57mm x 46mm. The short stroke is necessary to achieve high cranking speeds; and only this elevated rpm ceiling, which allows

the engine to combust great quantities of gasoline and air every second, has kept the MV Agusta in the same horsepower league with the two-strokes.

Great horsepower creates handling difficulties. The 1974 four-cylinder MV made at least ten horsepower more than the previous MV championship bike, a three-cylinder 500. Throughout the 1974 season MV experimented with frames having curved tubes, and others with straight-line members, and still others with subtle combinations. In the search to steady the 500 four's handling, MV even installed an idler sprocket on the lower chain run; theoretically the extra sprocket was supposed to damp out chain whip that could upset the handling. The legendary MV road holding gradually returned.

MV Agusta has no significant motorcycle production. Indeed, the company's business is the manufacture of helicopters, so MV does not race for commercial reasons. For this Italian concern, world championship road racing is a matter of love and honor.

MV 500's small size becomes apparent in the pit—and on the track with World Champion Phil Read in the saddle.

Yamaha YZR-350

Nowhere did Yamaha's battle plans succeed so brilliantly as in the 350 world championship series in road racing. The 350 water-cooled twins swept all adversaries away. The only serious opposition came from MV Agusta, which tried to match the Yamaha 350 twin with a four-cylinder four-stroke. So devastating were the Yamaha twins that the MV opposition was driven off. After early-season appearances, MV withdrew their 350 fours from world competition, leaving the title to an intramural fight between Yamaha riders Dieter Braun and Giacomo Agostini. In the end, reigning 350 World Champion Agostini prevailed on a works Yamaha.

The factory-supported 350cc twins were essentially refined TZ-350 production-racer Yamahas. The twin-cylinder, water-cooled factory bikes were significantly lighter than those machines sold to privateers, thanks to magnesium crankcases, lightweight frames, and other special bits. Some paddock tipsters claimed the works Yamaha 350's had been shaved back to 250 pounds. The six-speed factory bikes never lacked power, with 72–76 horsepower on tap from 11,500-rpm engines. Those figures produced a power-to-weight ratio which was close to that of Yamaha's 500cc four-cylinder grand prix racer.

The 350 twin has benefited from three years of development. First used in Europe in 1972, the water-cooled TZ-350 arrived in private hands early in 1973. After a long period of steady improvement, the engine has probably reached its final stage; lap times can be dropped further only by working on weight reduction and handling refinements. Which is exactly the path Yamaha followed in 1974.

Though the fortunes of grand prix wars change season to season, the **142** fully developed Yamaha twin holds its world crown more firmly than any other victor in international road racing.

YZR-350, similar to, but distinct
from, the production TZ-350 Yamaha, powered
Giacomo Agostini to another championship.

Harley-Davidson 250

After more than a decade, the Italians returned the 250 World Championship in Road Racing to Italy. The last 250 title won by an Italian on Italian equipment occurred in 1960. Thereafter, the golden age of Japanese power—Honda and Yamaha—began. The best 250 Italian showing came in 1969 when Australian Kel Carruthers won the lightweight crown on an Italian Benelli. So Walter Villa's victory on the Harley-Davidson/AerMacchi in 1974 capped a long struggle.

The Harley-Davidson two-stroke racer first splashed into the center of international racing in 1972 when Renzo Pasolini finished second in world class competition. This early air-cooled version gave way to a water-cooled model in 1973. A year later, the Italian racing 250 sported twin disc brakes. The slow pace of development always left the Latin twin trailing the Yamaha 250's by a half-step.

In 1974 Harley-Davidson caught up with Yamaha in Europe. The Italian and Japanese bikes are quite similar. Both are water-cooled, piston-port two-strokes with chrome-plated aluminum cylinders. Both bikes mix fuel and air with 34 Mikiuni carburetors. The Harley-Davidson controls the firing of spark plugs with an electronic triggering system. So does the Yamaha racer. Both bikes have six-speed gearboxes. The Harley-Davidson engine dimensions measure 56mm x 50mm, while the Yamaha remains perfectly square at 54mm x 54mm. The Italian racer will rev a little harder (12,000 rpm) than the Yamaha. With about 55 horsepower on tap, both the Harley-Davidson and Yamaha can pierce the 150-mph barrier.

Given the similarities between the two racers, only superior organization, greater determination, and harder riding by Villa gave the Italians the 250 world title.

145

The Harley-Davidson racer, like other works two-strokes, has the power characteristics of a light-switch: all-on or all-off.

Yamaha YZ-623

Defending champions in the 125cc class, Kent Andersson and the 125 Grand Prix Yamaha, squeaked out another world title in 1974. Like the 500 and 350 classes, the hotly contested 125 championship hung undecided until the close of the season. In fact the 125 World Championship in Road Racing proved uncertain until the last corner of the last lap of the final grand prix race of the year.

At the Czechoslovakian Grand Prix, the year-long tussle between Yamaha and the Italian Morbidelli came to settlement. The Italian pilot, Paola Pileri—who was racing with a broken collarbone—had Andersson's Yamaha well covered. Then the Morbidelli coughed and sputtered to a stop in the final corner. Pileri had run out of gas! His nearly clinched title escaped. Andersson won.

FIM rules for the 125 class limit manufacturers to engines with two cylinders and gearboxes with six speeds. Therefore all 125 racers line up in a general pattern: water-cooled twin-cylinder two-stroke engines, electronic ignition systems, dry clutches, lightweight running gear, and super-efficient streamlining.

The 125 Grand Prix Yamaha produces about 40 horsepower at 15,000 rpm. The machine weighs around 180 pounds, and its top speed ranges upward to 140 mph. The YZ-623 employs piston-port induction and draws its mixture through two 26mm carburetors. Both the Italian Morbidelli and Spanish Derbi have rotary-valve induction systems, a more complex set-up which has great horsepower potential—in theory at least.

Nevertheless, racing is more than a set of blueprints. Even luck has **146** its place, as Kent Andersson will acknowledge.

Under the plumbing live two tiny 60cc cylinders. The large canister is the oil-trap bottle for the breather system.

Van Veen Kreidler

Continental motorcycle enthusiasts sustain the 50cc World Championship. The tiddler class shrivelled and died in England after enjoying brief popularity in the 1960's. And 50cc racing never came alive in the United States. But on the Continent, the Dutch, the Spanish, and the Germans form the backbone of 50cc racing. Kreidler, Jamathi, and Derbi all field impressive machinery.

The FIM formula for the 50cc road-racing class mandates single-cylinder engines and six-speed gearboxes. These limitations keep the machines relatively simple and encourage small manufacturers to participate. Major contenders include German Kreidlers, Spanish Derbis, and Dutch Jamathis. Van Veen, the Kreidler importers for the Netherlands, also constitutes a major force. Aboard the Van Veen Kreidler, Henk van Kessel won the 1974 50cc World Championship in Road Racing.

The Van Veen racer has a water-cooled, disc-valve, two-stroke engine. The powerplant develops about 19–20 horsepower with a piston the size of a bourbon shot-glass. The 26mm carburetor is nearly the size of the cylinder. The power peak occurs at 16,000 rpm, but a knife-edged powerband will not do. Six-speed gearboxes force a fairly wide spread of power. Every ounce of output must go a long way, so Van Veen Kreidlers are very light: 125 pounds. The tiny machines require small riders who won't overwhelm the fragile bikes. All 50cc racers look as if they have been stretched (and lowered) like a piece of taffy.

Frail appearances should not imply sluggish racers. At the Belgian Grand Prix held at Spa-Francorchamps, the fastest 50cc mighty mites can lap the course at an average speed of almost 100 mph. The maximum top speed for the Van Veen Kreidler is dazzling: 127-plus mph!

Though he's not a giant, World Champion Henk van Kessel dwarfs the tiny Van Veen Kreidler.

Zundapp 125 MX

As the most recent addition to the world championship schedule in motocross, the 125cc class continues to gain momentum. The world-title chase has already attracted European factories, including Zundapp, Bultaco, Montesa, and Husqvarna. Though no Japanese manufacturer has begun a full assault on the title, that time approaches rapidly.

In 1974 the age of super-special factory racers had not arrived in the 125cc class. The young Belgian rider, André Malherbe, claimed the title on a Zundapp—a production-line motocrosser which appeared almost disgustingly standard. Indeed, the motorcycle had a very heavy steel frame and production-stock wheels. Zundapp did not bother to craft the gas tank or fenders in super-light plastic. The tank was common steel; the fenders, aluminum. Nothing special distinguished the front fork. And only late in the season did Koni shock absorbers replace the Girling units. Zundapp offered no dazzling suspension tricks. The rear dampers were canted just slightly forward, and the German factory didn't use any large-capacity, long-travel shocks.

Malherbe's engine, however, really performed. The all-aluminum engine had a special high-compression cylinderhead and a 30mm Amal carburetor. With some porting changes and its six-speed transmission, the Zundapp was the fastest, quickest bike in the 125 world class.

So much stronger was the German engine, some competitors mumbled that the Zunnie must be a 150cc or 175cc engine. Yet no one had enough confidence in that theory to protest the winning machine. Thus, the "big engine" talk amounted to a backhanded compliment for the super-power 125 Zundapp and its equally potent rider, André Malherbe.

150

Whether aviating or blasting out of the corner, the Zundapp 125 showed its superior power throughout the season.

KTM 250 MX

In 1974 Gennady Moiseev became the first Russian to win a world championship crown in motocross. The USSR rider battled all season aboard his Austrian KTM. His main adversary was Czechoslovakian Jaroslav Falta on a works CZ, and the last race decided the championship. Indeed, the title remained unsettled even after the event. Falta "won" the race; he had, however, jumped the start, and after the FIM jury assessed a time-penalty, Falta's placing fell from first to ninth. That descent erased the margin necessary to beat Moiseev. It was the Russian's day, and his championship.

Moiseev's grand prix bike was no Austro-Russian secret weapon. In fact, the machine had amazingly standard specifications, almost identical to the Penton (KTM) motocrossers sold over-the-counter in the United States. Luck and trick-machinery played no large part in Moiseev's success. He had winning talent—and so did his KTM.

Suspension tuning was a constant throughout the grand prix season. Early in the year, an Italian Marzocchi fork went on the KTM as a Ceriani fork came off. The Marzocchi fork legs had 8 inches of travel, and early versions were nitrogen-pressurized. At mid-season, Moiseev mounted experimental (Bilstein type) shock absorbers which had no springs whatever; gas controlled all rear suspension action. Seal failures prompted KTM to abandon the gas-only shocks and to switch to gas-filled Marzocchi rear dampers with springs. At the same time, the rear suspension configuration changed from a forward-mount shock system to a cantilever position.

If KTM did a fair amount of experimentation with the suspension, the firm left the engine department virtually untouched. Moiseev tried very minor changes in tune, but he retained the stock engine with its 36mm Bing carburetor. And why not? KTM bikes were the fastest 250's all year on the grand prix circuit.

153

Massive cylinder and cylinderhead completely dominate the engine bay of Moiseev's KTM 250.

Husqvarna 360 Grand Prix

Heikki Mikkola captured the 500cc World Championship in Motocross from the saddle of a Swedish Husqvarna. A development of the 1973 GP bike, the 1974 Husqvarna had different cylinder castings which produced various states of tune. At the start of the 1974 European season, the Husky engine had a very pipey kind of horsepower. In fact, the engine was so peaky that the motorcycle was hard to ride: with so much sudden power, the rear wheel spun easily and traction vanished.

Husqvarna tamed the vicious power characteristics by altering port-window shapes and fitting a larger flywheel magneto. A bored-out 38mm Bing carburetor matched the porting demands nicely. The power fed directly into a small, all-steel clutch and thence through the six-speed transmission. With cases cast in magnesium, the engine contri-

buted to the motocrosser's lightness—215 pounds at the season's end.

While Husqvarna sorted out the engine, there was much progress with the running gear. An early frame change dropped the engine elevation and lowered the center of gravity. Shortly thereafter, the factory lengthened the swing arm and heavily gusseted the chrome-moly frame to withstand the stresses imposed by the forward-mounted shock absorbers. Mikkola first tried Bilstein gas dampers, but later he permanently switched to new Girling gas-oil units. By the close of the season, rear-wheel travel reached 8.5 inches with laydown shocks, and the front wheel had over 8 inches of suspension movement.

In 1974 Husqvarna's grand prix bikes had built-in toughness. Heikki Mikkola demonstrated that point well—for he rides with pounding savagery. His style may lack perfect grace, but no one can quarrel with his effectiveness.   **155**

Hardware alone won't win a grand
prix motocross; riders like Mikkola are
great athletes in superb condition.

Yamaha YZR-500

Yamaha intended to chase the Italians out of the 500 World Championship in Road Racing. The Japanese planned a two-pronged attack. First, they hired Giacomo Agostini—who had won thirteen world championships on MV Agustas—away from the Italian concern. Second, Yamaha went to the grand prix wars with fabulous racing equipment.

By a narrow margin, Yamaha failed to make Agostini the 500 World Champion again. Technically, however, the four-cylinder Yamaha 500 won the constructor's title, though the Japanese factory refused to accept the prize. Major grand prix stars, and the official MV and Yamaha teams, boycotted the German Grand Prix in 1974 as a protest against hazardous riding conditions. A private Yamaha won the German Grand Prix, which—despite the boycott—officially counted toward the world title. In this way Yamaha won the manufacturer's award. But in a demonstration of gentlemanly sportsmanship, Yamaha refused the title, since the German event had not been won by an official factory Yamaha.

Yamaha, winner in absentia, did battle with a transverse 500cc four-cylinder engine. Originally, the piston-port two-stroke engine was just a smaller version of the water-cooled TZ-700 Yamaha road racer. As the grand prix season unfolded, Yamaha unveiled a lighter, narrower version of the 500 which produced 93 horsepower. But Yamaha concentrated on frame design more than engine tweaking. This soon became apparent when Yamaha introduced a frame which had a cantilever rear swinging arm controlled by a large damper and spring. This shock absorber mounted under the fuel tank and anchored to the steering head.

At first the frame and engine enjoyed great success. Yamaha reputedly trimmed the weight down to 300 pounds—or slightly less. Despite its outstanding credentials, little problems plagued the bike; and these setbacks, together with the normal misfortunes of racing, upset the grand Yamaha plan in the 500 class. That was too bad—because Yamaha brought the first burst of technical innovations in a generation of 500-class racing.

157

*Most distinctive feature
of the YZR-500 is its mono-shock
cantilever rear suspension.*

Index

Add to your
KNOWLEDGE
THROUGH
COLOR

(All Books $1.45 Each)
(Where marked • $1.95 Each)

Listed on the opposite page are the currently available titles in this paperback series. To add to your KNOWLEDGE THROUGH COLOR library, simply list the books you want and mail to:

BANTAM BOOKS, INC.
Dept. KTC-1
666 Fifth Avenue
New York, N.Y. 10019

Add 25¢ to your order to cover postage and handling. Please send a check or money order, since we cannot be responsible for orders containing cash.

A BANTAM CATALOG IS AVAILABLE UPON REQUEST.
Just send your name and address and 10¢ (to help defray postage and handling costs) to: Catalog Department, Bantam Books, Inc., 414 East Golf Road, Des Plaines, Illinois 60016.